The Future of Energy Digitalization and Financial Reshaping

Compiled and Written by Yang Lei

Translated by Luo Yonghua, Cao Xiaofei

I0490051

Paris Agreement, Blue Sky Defense Campaign, Energy Transition, Energy in Turbulent Changes

Energy Digitalization, Energy Internet, Energy Services, Digital Transformation of Energy

New Practices in Energy Trading, Blockchain's Reach in Energy, The Invisible Hand of Finance

Energy Market-oriented Reform and Industrial Adjustment: Where Are We Heading?

CHICAGO ACADEMIC PRESS

The Future of Energy
Digitalization and Financial Reshaping
Author: Yang Lei
Translator: Luo Yonghua and Cao Xiaofei
Language: English
Word Count: Approximately 127,000 words
Publisher: Chicago Academic Press
Number of Pages: 200
ISBN: 978-1-965890-95-0

Publishing   Chicago Academic Press

              5923 N Artesian Ave

              Chicago IL 60659

Email   contact@chicagoacademicpress.com

Website   http://chicagoacademicpress.com/

Book Size   6X9 inches

First Edition November, 2025

Author's Profile

Yang Lei, Ph.D., was born in May 1974. He is a researcher at the Institute of Energy, Peking University, a member of the Academic Committee of the Research Center for Energy Transition and Social Development at the School of Social Sciences, Tsinghua University, and the deputy director of the Editorial Board of *International Petroleum Economics*. He has successively held positions such as the Senior Advisor to the Executive Director of the International Energy Agency; the division director and deputy director-general at the National Development; and Reform Commission and the National Energy Administration.tion. He is committed to promoting energy transition, energy reform, and global energy governance, has participated in the research and formulation of a number of energy policies, and is enthusiastic about public awareness efforts in the energy field.

Translator Profile

Luo Yonghua, male, born in 1979 in Yongxing, Hunan, holds a PhD and is a professor. He is a member of the Guangdong Provincial Thousand and Ten Project and a member of the Teaching Guidance Committee for Logistics Management and Engineering majors in undergraduate universities in Guangdong Province. His main research areas include regional economy, labor economy, and port logistics.He started teaching at Guangdong University of Petrochemical Technology in August 2005 and currently serves as the Dean of the School of Economics and Management. He presided over or participated in more than 20 national, provincial and ministerial projects, presided over and completed 7 horizontal projects of enterprises and institutions, and published 50 papers in important journals such as Financial Research, among which 2 were reprinted in full by Renmin University of China. Edited or co edited 3 textbooks, published 1 book, and wrote multiple decision-making consulting reports that received approval from the main leaders of the Maoming Municipal Party Committee and Municipal Government. Won one second prize in the Education and Teaching Achievement Award of the China Petroleum Education Society; Won 2 first prizes, 1 second prize, and 1 third prize for excellent papers at the Guangdong Provincial Social Science Academic Annual Conference, 2 first prizes for good journal works in Chongqing, and 2 second prizes and 2 third prizes for excellent achievements in philosophy and social sciences in Maoming City.

Cao Xiaofei, born in Yongxing, Hunan in 1980, is a Ph.D., professor, and master's supervisor at Renmin University of China. He is also the Vice Dean of the School of Marxism at Guangdong University of Petrochemical Technology, a target of the "Thousand and Ten Talents Project" in Guangdong Province, and the head of the "Ideological and Political Course Master Studio" in Maoming City. Mainly engaged in research on national security and international issues, has led more than 10 provincial and ministerial level projects such as the National Social Science Fund and the Ministry of Education Social Science Fund, and has published over 40 papers in journals such as "Introduction to Ideological and Theoretical Education", "South Asian Studies Quarterly", and "Southeast Asia Vertical and Horizontal". Received 2 second prizes and 3 third prizes for provincial-level teaching and research achievements, 2 second prizes for municipal level teaching and research achievements, and 2 first prizes for school level teaching and research achievements.

Email: cxf8077@163.com

Abstract

This book uses accessible language to introduce the situation and development trends faced by the global energy transition. As people's awareness improves and lifestyles change, a greener and more environmentally friendly energy system is no longer just a vision but increasingly a necessity. Through a large number of specific domestic and international practices, the book expounds on the progress of the "Third Industrial Revolution" in the energy sector and introduces the application of blockchain technology in energy and energy finance. It also looks ahead to the new landscape these changes will bring to the future energy system. This book can serve as a reference for the public to understand and participate in energy transition and related policy-making, as well as a guide for investors to grasp trends and take concrete actions.

Library of Congress Cataloging-in-Publication Data (CIP Data)

Preface

The importance of energy is beyond doubt. For a long time, from the perspective of the general public, energy production has been perceived as the domain of a few large corporations and nations—a field controlled by a select few. However, this situation is undergoing significant changes, increasingly felt by all: the shale oil and gas revolution has transformed the global energy supply and demand landscape; the rapid development of renewable energy has made it competitive with traditional energy sources; energy intelligence has fostered a growing number of energy prosumers (producers and consumers); electric vehicles (EVs) are rising at an astonishing pace; more and more information technology companies are entering the energy sector; and finance is playing an increasingly prominent role in the energy field...

In his renowned bestseller, *The Third Industrial Revolution*, published in 2011, Jeremy Rifkin predicted numerous scenarios for the future of energy, particularly highlighting the transformative changes brought about by the integration of the internet and renewable energy. Looking back nine years later, many of these advancements have occurred even faster than depicted in his book. When President Xi Jinping proposed the energy revolution in 2014, many might have struggled to understand why such a strong term as "revolution" was used instead of the milder "reform." Over the past five years, the landscape of the energy revolution has become clearer globally and in China, depicting not only institutional changes but also a revolutionary energy future.

When discussing the future of energy, despite differing inclinations among specific industries within the energy sector, a fundamental consensus has emerged: energy will evolve towards diversification, cleanliness, low carbonization, intelligence, decentralization, electrification, marketization, and democratization. Dr. Chen Xinhua, President of the Beijing International Energy Experts Club, summarized the driving forces behind energy transformation into seven "Ds", using the initial letters of English words, while Dr. Zhai Yongping, Energy Director at the Asian Development Bank, proposed that the direction of energy transformation should have clear standards: reducing emissions and being people-oriented, ultimately focusing on the latter, as emission reduction also aims at the future of humanity. Industry insiders are clear-minded about the direction of energy transformation, but much of the impetus for change comes from external sources.

Since energy entered modern society, a primary reason for considering energy security as a crucial issue has been resource constraints. Possessing energy resources equates to strategic initiative and even victory in wars. In the past, people often worried about the arrival of "peak oil," referring to the production peak due to resource constraints. However, in recent years, discussions about "peak oil" have shifted to when oil consumption will peak, with oil companies now expressing concern. Resource constraints are increasingly giving way to technology; with the right technology, shale oil and gas production can be significantly increased economically; with the right technology, renewable energy can become cheaper than fossil fuels... Meanwhile, severe environmental issues such as climate change and air pollution have brought energy issues into sharper focus, with environmental constraints becoming the most significant external factor influencing energy development.

The growing external factors influencing energy do not end there. As with many industrial revolutions in the past one to two decades, the internet has disrupted numerous industries, with disruptors typically being so-called "outsiders." When examining the impact of the internet era on the energy industry, compared to other sectors, the influence has been relatively minor. For example, power plants have merely installed more advanced software systems and claimed to have completed digitalization. This is partly because the industry is vast and has significant inertia, requiring time to accumulate the strength for change, and partly because relevant preparations are not fully in place, with disruptors still emerging.

However, this force is accumulating; and a sense of impending change is palpable. Two key forces are maturing: one is digitization, which essentially transforms the traditional energy system through the internet and related thinking; the other is the reshaping role of finance.

Energy digitization is both a result of digital technology development and an inevitable requirement for energy advancement. Increasingly, renewable energy sources like wind and solar are unstable providers and require flexible coupling with the system to avoid waste and enhance value. Rapidly growing distributed energy sources also demand more real-time allocation to achieve supply-demand balance. The broad prospects of smart homes, including electric vehicles, also require digital support. In this process, increasingly flexible market mechanisms increase energy arbitrage opportunities, necessitating digitization for transactions, with blockchain technology significantly reducing transaction costs. Some scholars refer to data as the oil of the 21st century. Klaus Schwab, founder of the World Economic Forum, also emphasizes that the core of the new industrial revolution is intelligence and informatization based on big data. Energy digitization enables cross-border integration, as Tesla claims to be strategically an information company rather than an automotive company, as it will integrate more resources. In fact, Tesla has already made a mark in the energy industry with its photovoltaic (PV) and energy storage solutions. Google, Apple, and others have also begun to make inroads into the energy sector.

In the energy revolution, finance will play a more significant role as an invisible driving force. Historically, the US dollar's long-standing strength as the world's currency has been closely tied to its link with oil. As energy enters a new development stage, finance will again interact closely with energy. A recent example is the success of the shale oil and gas revolution, a remarkable turnaround achieved by numerous small and medium-sized US enterprises with the help of financial capital. The shale oil and gas industry, supported by capital, continued to increase production despite continuous losses until achieving positive cash flow industry-wide in 2018. The shale oil and gas revolution's transformation of the global energy landscape has become an inspiring classic in the energy industry. This closely resembles the business logic of internet companies, where many new economy-driven enterprises also sustain losses for over a decade but see their market value increase due to rapid performance growth.

However, this is just the tip of the iceberg in terms of the alliance between finance and energy. The decentralization and digitization of energy have enabled blockchain technology to emerge in the energy sector. The Brooklyn Microgrid Project in New York is experimenting with blockchain technology for real-time settlement among local energy prosumers and ambitiously aims to expand this model. Global practices of energy virtual currencies are springing up like mushrooms, with State Grid's Electric Vehicle Service Company developing "Lvdou" (Green Beans) in the lab, linked to electricity trading, to build a new energy trading model.

In June 2019, Facebook released a white paper announcing its intention to launch its virtual currency, "Libra." This event attracted global attention and was seen as a turning point for virtual electronic currencies.

How Libra will connect with real-world assets or fiat currencies (such as the US dollar) has also become a focal point of discussion. Just as the US dollar's link with oil solidified its position as an international currency, Libra's most realistic option remains energy, the largest commodity in global trade by volume. However, this time it will not be limited to oil or natural gas but will encompass all energy sources linked to calorific value. This process will take time and require interaction with regulators, inevitably encountering obstacles, but the trend is already evident.

This tidal wave is unstoppable. After years of gestation, the technology is mature, costs are decreasing at an unprecedented pace, and business models and policies are rapidly evolving in this direction. This process will involve fierce competition among major countries, but also requires more cooperation. As the world's largest energy consumer, China is deeply advancing its energy revolution, but it clearly lacks a head start in many areas. How to plan is a critical and challenging issue.

Ultimately, both energy and finance should serve humanity, with a people-centered focus, create a better life, and enhance human happiness. Any industrial revolution involving significant changes will be accompanied by many growing pains, including the decline of traditional industries, the anxiety of new industries, and the emergence of many speculators, even those fantasizing about ruling the world in new ways. The occurrence and progress of the new energy revolution require the joint participation and promotion of visionaries, a process that demands not only

a long-term perspective but also an inclusive mindset.

Contents

The end of the Stone Age did not come because stones ran out. Similarly, the advent of the new energy era is not due to the depletion of fossil fuels.

Modern energy has evolved alongside the Industrial Revolution, transitioning from coal to oil and gas, and now to new energy sources, constantly shifting from high-carbon to low-carbon. Energy transformation is also a part of the Industrial Revolution. With the deepening of the Third Industrial Revolution, Regarding the classification of industrial revolution stages, different scholars adopt varying criteria. Some propose that we have now entered the Fourth Industrial Revolution. This book follows the classification standard in Rifkin's The Third Industrial Revolution, considering the current stage as one of synergistic development between the information industry and new energy. A massive wave of energy transformation is surging ahead.

The primary constraint on energy development is no longer resources but the environment and emissions. Climate change poses the greatest threat to the environment, with extreme weather and air pollution presenting more immediate dangers to humanity than resource depletion. According to the requirements of the Paris Agreement, the time we have left is very limited.

Clear waters and lush mountains are invaluable assets. After years of extensive development, people have finally realized the heavy toll of high-energy-consuming economic growth. The environment will serve as a rigid constraint on energy development, making clean and low-carbon energy an inevitable requirement.

The local nature of renewable energy enables everyone to become an energy-producing consumer (prosumer). Distributed energy blurs the lines between energy production and consumption. With the help of digitization, peer-to-peer transactions are forming new business models, which will drive the restructuring of the entire energy system from the demand side.

The cost reduction of new energy, represented by photovoltaics, has far exceeded expectations. Technological progress is driving industrial upgrading, with technology replacing resources as the primary guarantee of energy security. Once technology achieves commercial breakthroughs, it will inevitably lead to explosive growth. The gray rhino is already on the horizon.

Advances and cost reductions in battery storage have provided a strong impetus for the development of electric vehicles. By 2030, China is expected to have hundreds of millions of EVs. If these EVs were to charge simultaneously, the required installed capacity could exceed the current total installed capacity of China. On one hand, EVs will impact the electricity market; on the other hand, they could serve as flexible virtual peaking power plants. As an alternative technological route, green hydrogen produced from renewable energy offers vast possibilities, not only powering fuel cells but also replacing fossil fuels in sectors such as steel, chemicals, and heating, further breaking down barriers between energy sources.

Digital technology has profoundly changed our lives, but its impact on energy is just beginning to unfold, with its power accumulating and poised to drive energy from mere supply to comprehensive service, a substantive manifestation of the energy revolution.

With a significant decline in information technology costs, energy digitization has gradually taken shape. Digitization is not just a corporate initiative but has also become a government and national strategy. This wave of digitization in the energy industry lays the foundation for deeper digitalization of the entire energy system.

Non-traditional energy companies like Google and Tesla are making significant inroads into the energy sector, equipping new energy with internet thinking and cutting-edge AI technologies, differing greatly from traditional energy companies. The gray rhino of the energy industrial revolution has begun to stir up dust.

Rifkin's vision of the Energy Internet envisions "a renewable energy-based, distributed, open, and shared network." More than a physical framework design, the Energy Internet represents a new energy development philosophy. This concept has received strong support from the Chinese government and industry, surpassing many Western countries with more favorable development conditions.

The energy industry is transforming into a service industry, with the boundaries between different energy sources blurring. Industry giants have recognized this trend; ENGIE sold its upstream natural gas assets to focus on energy services, while China's State Grid has also embraced energy services as its flagship initiative. Energy services represent a demand-driven supply-side revolution, centered on improving energy efficiency and providing higher-quality, personalized services. Can traditional energy companies make this transition?

Energy has always been closely linked to finance, not only because it is a capital-intensive industry, but also because finance is actively influencing energy development. In the future, blockchain technology will forge new energy currencies, a trend already emerging.

The link between oil and the US dollar has solidified the dollar's status as a global "hard currency." In the new century, Wall Street's support for shale companies' financing resembles an internet model, helping these companies weather prolonged losses. The success of the shale oil and gas revolution is not just an energy industry triumph but also a financial industry achievement. Green finance is becoming a trend, but the revolution brought about by the fusion of finance and energy is only just beginning.

In the spring of 2016, when a Brooklyn neighborhood in New York adopted blockchain technology to build an Energy Internet community, it marked the first real-world use of virtual currency for peer-to-peer energy trading, quickly demonstrating its vitality. Various energy tokens have emerged in global energy markets, further linking energy and finance.

Since its inception, blockchain has had a profound impact, first gaining prominence in finance and quickly expanding into various fields. In energy, it has shown strong vitality in applications ranging from trading platforms and energy tokens to EV charging, green certificate tracking, energy asset management, and peer-to-peer transactions.

Blockchain will serve as the adhesive between energy and finance. The release of Facebook's Libra virtual currency white paper sparked global attention, with both enthusiastic support and fierce opposition. The future combination of distributed energy and virtual currencies supported by blockchain technology is inevitable, resembling the partnership between oil and the dollar. However, this time, it heralds a brand-new era.

Chinese energy industry leaders and government officials have demonstrated remarkable vision and insight, being among the earliest advocates of the Energy Internet globally. In practice, building an Energy Internet and responding to financial reshaping require an open market system as a prerequisite. Without an open energy market, real-time response to price signals—a prerequisite for various business model innovations—cannot be achieved. From this perspective, understanding President Xi's "Four Revolutions and One Cooperation" highlights the enormous challenges we face.

Energy, finance, and the internet are undoubtedly crucial topics, but without serving humanity and improving people's well-being, they lose their fundamental purpose. The tide of innovation inevitably brings about industrial rise and fall, fostering vitality on one hand while affecting millions of livelihoods on the other. In this journey, staying true to our original aspirations is particularly important.

Part I

The Turbulent Rise of Energy

The end of the Stone Age did not come because stones ran out. Similarly, the advent of the new energy era is not due to the depletion of fossil fuels.

Ahmed Zaki Yamani served as Saudi Arabia's Minister of Petroleum from 1962 to 1986. During this period, he repeatedly wielded the weapon of oil embargoes, including the 1973 oil embargo that dealt a heavy blow to the United States. Using oil as his leverage, he maneuvered adeptly in the international energy arena and dominated the international oil market for over two decades. Now, more than thirty years have passed, and those remarkable achievements have faded into oblivion. Most people no longer remember his former role, and even his name has gradually been forgotten. However, one of his quotes has been widely circulated: "The Stone Age did not end for lack of stone, and the Oil Age will end not for lack of oil." Spoken by the Petroleum Minister of Saudi Arabia, these words carry a certain ironic undertone. At the time, he made this statement to justify Saudi Arabia's decision not to cut oil production, yet it sounded remarkably forward-looking. As the new century dawned and the embryonic form of the third industrial revolution, represented by new energy sources, began to emerge, revisiting his words gives them a prophetic tone. Moreover, it can be further expanded upon to say: The advent of the new energy era is not due to the depletion of fossil fuels.

Energy Transition

Humanity's entry into the Industrial Revolution era through the use of fossil fuels spans just over two centuries. Within this relatively short period, energy has undergone at least three major transitions, and the process continues. This evolution is driven not only by the continuous discovery of new energy resources but also by the changing industrial demands and external constraints as industrial revolutions progress, resulting from the dynamic interaction between energy, industry, and the environment.

These three energy revolutions can be roughly delineated by coal, oil and gas, and new energy sources, corresponding respectively to the first two industrial revolutions represented by steam engines and internal combustion engines, and the third industrial revolution characterized by modern power electronics and the internet. Jeremy Rifkin, in his book *The Third Industrial Revolution*, clearly defines the five pillars of the third industrial revolution, each directly related to energy. He posits that the decentralized use of renewable energy combined with internet technology represents a significant manifestation of this revolution. Technologies associated with the energy transition, such as smart grids, electric vehicles, energy Internet of Things, mobile energy storage stations, and blockchain, are not reliant on specific primary energy sources but are primarily characterized by data-driven intelligence, potentially exerting a profound impact on the energy industry and human society at large.

While there is a consensus on the trend of energy transition, experts may hold varying preferences. According to Robert Hefner III, a renowned American energy futurist, he categorizes energy into solid, liquid, and gaseous forms, naming the third energy era the "Gas Age." He envisions natural gas playing a dominant role in the short term, with hydrogen and renewable energy taking the lead in the future. He includes all renewable energy sources within the Gas Age, viewing wind energy, for instance, as a form of gaseous motion. This perspective might be influenced by his family's ownership of a natural gas company, reflecting a bias towards natural gas. Nevertheless, his early proposition of a grand energy transition has resonated widely and continues to manifest in practice.

The French have a proud saying: "We may lack oil, but we possess ideas." Similarly, Chinese Academy of Sciences Academician Zou Caineng has a notable quote with a similar sentiment: "Only thoughts can be exhausted, not energy sources." He believes that a world energy structure where coal, oil, natural gas, and new energy each hold a significant share is taking shape, marking a new phase of transition from coal and oil and gas to new energy.

From a broader perspective, energy is moving towards a cleaner and lower-carbon direction. Oil is less carbon-intensive than coal, natural gas even less so, and renewable energy sources are essentially carbon-free. In 1900, coal accounted for over half of global primary energy consumption;

by 2018, this share had declined to 27%. Although this transition has been uneven across different regions, with many developing countries pledging not to follow the "pollute first, clean up later" path taken by developed nations, there remains a strong reliance on the trajectory from high-carbon to low-carbon energy sources. Overall, the foundation of human industrial civilization's reliance on fossil fuels remains unchanged, with approximately 80% of global energy still derived from fossil fuels even in the new century (Figure 1-1).

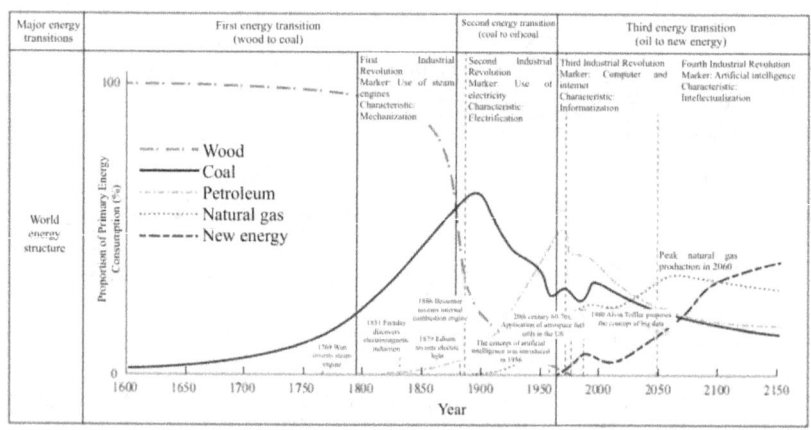

Figure 1-1 Evolution and Forecast of Global Primary Energy Composition (Source: *New Energy*)

In the second decade of the 21st century, more revolutionary changes have occurred. According to tracking statistics from the International Energy Agency (IEA), over the eight years starting from 2008, the average cost of photovoltaic power has decreased by about 80%, wind power by about 70%, and energy storage by about 70%. Meanwhile, costs for broadband, sensors, and wireless data have plummeted by over 95% (Figure 1-2). On one hand, such rapid cost reductions have opened up vast prospects for the commercialization of new energy sources; on the other hand, the pressure to reduce carbon dioxide emissions to combat climate change poses unprecedented challenges to traditional energy sources.

The year 2008 is set as 100

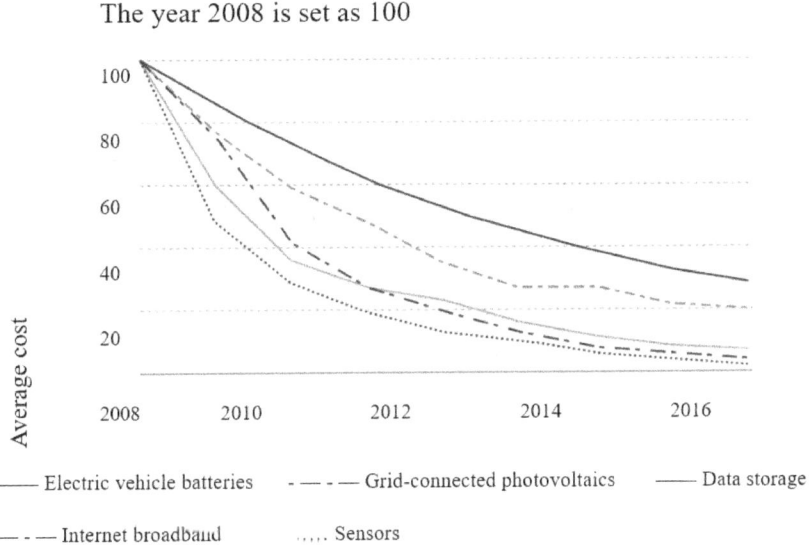

Figure 1-2 Reduction in the average costs of relevant energy technologies (Source: IEA)

According to IEA statistics, from 2012 to 2017, the growth in new thermal power generation capacity halved, while the growth in new renewable energy power generation capacity tripled. Looking ahead to 2023, PV and wind power are expected to account for more than half of all new power generation capacity (Figure 1-3). In early 2019, the International Renewable Energy Agency (IRENA) released its latest report, stating that

7

global renewable energy capacity already accounts for one-third of total installed capacity, with PV and wind power experiencing the fastest growth. After years of preparation, a new energy era is dawning.

Simultaneously, with the application of new technologies, energy efficiency continues to improve, and energy consumption per unit of GDP decreases annually. In other words, the same amount of energy consumption can generate increasingly larger outputs (Figure 1-4).

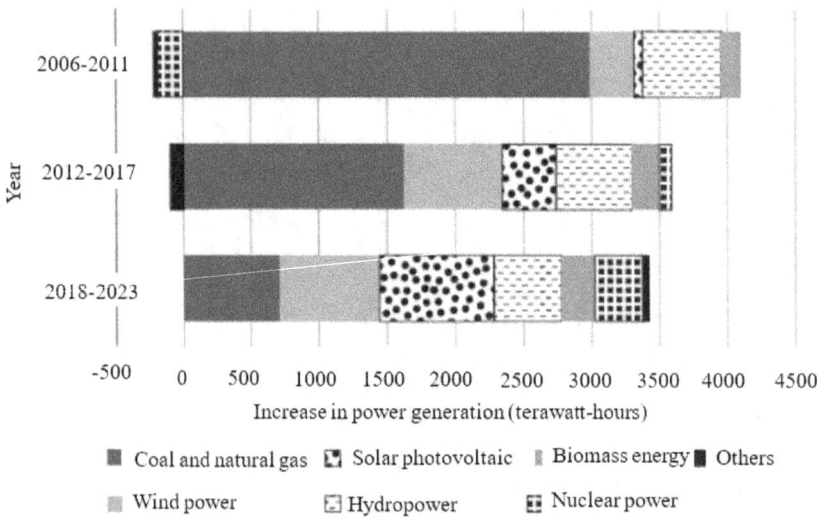

Figure 1-3 Sources of Global Newly Added Power Generation Capacity

(Source: IEA)

Note: After the Fukushima nuclear accident, nuclear power decreased, so the increment is negative.

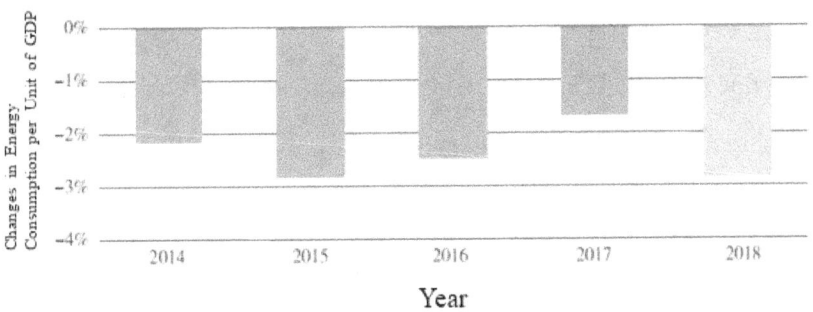

Figure 1-4 Chart of Changes in Energy Consumption Intensity

(Source: IEA)

The integration of different energy sources also contributes to enhancing overall system efficiency. For a long time, energy has been a relatively fragmented concept, as evidenced by its various units of measurement. Electricity is measured in kilowatt-hours, oil in barrels or liters, natural gas in cubic meters or million British thermal units, and coal in tons. Converting between these units can be a headache even for experts, let alone laypeople. This fragmentation is related to the long-standing sectoral divisions within the energy industry, with different energy enterprises having limited knowledge of each other and government departments managing energy in a siloed manner, each actively supporting their respective sectors without much consideration for optimizing the entire energy system.

With the increasing proportion of electricity in final consumption and the vigorous advancement of "re-electrification," the integration and substitution among various energy sources are strengthening. In Europe, natural gas and electricity have demonstrated excellent interactivity, with the principle of "using gas where appropriate and electricity where appropriate." The development of hydrogen energy further elevates this integration capability and expectations to new heights. For consumers, the source of heating—whether from electricity, natural gas, coal, or ground-source heat pumps—is inconsequential as long as it is stable and economical. The application of digital technologies has also unprecedentedly combined various energy categories in a more optimized manner, enabling a cleaner and more efficient energy supply.

In January 2017, shortly before stepping down as U.S. President, Barack Obama published a signed article *The Irreversible Momentum of Clean Energy* in the prestigious journal *Science*. He elaborated that from 2008 to 2015, while the U.S. economy grew by 10%, energy consumption decreased by 2.5%, implying an 11% reduction in energy intensity (energy consumption per unit of GDP) and an 18% reduction in carbon dioxide emissions per unit of GDP, achieving a "decoupling" of economic growth from energy consumption growth. He particularly emphasized that the development of clean energy and economic growth are not contradictory but have become a global trend, which not only mitigates global climate change but also brings economic benefits to the United States. While expressing these views, he also voiced concerns about his successor, Donald Trump, potentially withdrawing from *the Paris Agreement*.

The Paris Agreement

Nowadays, there are increasing reports about climate warming and extreme weather, which many people have experienced firsthand. Climate change has emerged as the greatest threat to the Earth's environment, posing a more immediate danger to humanity than resource depletion and acting as a sword of Damocles hanging over energy development.

In this global village, the most pressing real-world challenge is not an alien invasion, but climate change. Even though some experts and politicians continue to debate the causes of climate change, the catastrophic consequences of global climate change on humanity and ecosystems are undeniable: extreme weather events, glacial melting, permafrost thawing, coral reef death, rising sea levels, ecosystem alterations, increased droughts and floods, and deadly heatwaves, among others. These changes are no longer just predictions by scientists. From the Arctic to the equator, humanity is struggling to survive under the impact of global climate change, an undeniable fact.

In places like Paris, known for its mild climate with warm winters and cool summers, the longstanding habit of not installing air conditioners—and even the scarcity of electric fans in stores—is changing. In recent years, prolonged summer heatwaves have frequently resulted in fatalities.

This is merely the prelude to the impacts of climate change. We are currently experiencing dangerous climate change, with the wheel of warming spinning faster and faster. Studies by climatologists and geologists have shown that the Earth's climate has indeed undergone significant changes. Since the end of the last ice age, when humans emerged, the Earth's climate has remained relatively stable in a state familiar to current human populations for ten thousand years.

In March 2019, the World Meteorological Organization (WMO) released a new global climate report, in which Secretary-General Petteri Taalas stated that the period from 2015 to 2018 witnessed record-breaking global warming, leading to rising sea levels and melting ice at the North and South Poles, a trend that continued in 2019. In early 2019, Europe experienced record-high winter temperatures, North America suffered abnormally cold conditions, and Australia faced severe heatwaves. The extent of ice cover at the North and South Poles was again significantly below average.

According to *CNN*, on August 2, 2019, alone, 12.5 billion tons of ice melted in Greenland, marking the largest single-day melt on record and serving as a clear warning of the worsening climate crisis. Josh Willis, an oceanographer at NASA, said, "Greenland has enough ice to raise sea levels by 7.5 meters, which would be devastating for coastlines worldwide. The billions of tons of ice melting here will raise sea levels in Australia, Southeast Asia, the United States, and Europe."

The Earth's temperature is determined by the balance between the solar radiation absorbed by the Earth's surface and the infrared radiation emitted by the heated Earth into space. Over the long term, the energy absorbed by the Earth from the sun must balance with the radiation energy emitted by the Earth and its atmosphere into space. Atmospheric water vapor, carbon dioxide, and other trace gases such as methane, ozone, and fluorocarbons allow short-wave radiation from the sun to pass through the Earth's atmosphere with little attenuation but absorb long-wave radiation emitted by the Earth, preventing heat from escaping. These gases, therefore, have a greenhouse-like effect and are known as "greenhouse gases." By absorbing long-wave radiation, greenhouse gases reduce the net energy emission into outer space, causing the atmosphere and the Earth's surface to warm up—a phenomenon known as the "greenhouse effect." Nearly 30 gases that contribute to the greenhouse effect have been identified in the atmosphere, with carbon dioxide playing the most significant role, and methane, fluorocarbons, and nitrous oxide also playing considerable roles.

A more frightening prospect of global warming is that once it exceeds a certain threshold, it may enter a positive feedback stage, similar to electronic self-excitation, accelerating the deterioration. Climate warming will lead to reduced reflection from ice surfaces and significant methane leakage from permafrost. As sea ice melts faster, the ocean's ability to reflect solar radiation weakens, and the upper ocean absorbs more heat, causing the Arctic climate to warm at a faster rate than the global average. This, in turn, will alter ocean currents, significantly impacting coastal climates.

Large amounts of methane and carbon dioxide are sealed within the permafrost in regions such as Russia, Canada, and northern Europe, remaining frozen since before human existence. Much methane is stored in the form of combustible ice, with an estimated conversion rate of 1 cubic meter of combustible ice to 164 cubic meters of natural gas. Once released, the scenario will be explosive. There are no precise figures on the amount of methane in the permafrost, with estimates ranging from trillions to quadrillions of cubic meters—an astonishing quantity. Methane's greenhouse gas effect is much stronger than that of carbon dioxide. Once released in large quantities due to permafrost thawing, it will be like awakening a dormant demon. These greenhouse gases will further accelerate global warming, and the warming process will, in turn, expedite the release of these gases, leading to an irreversible process and disasters akin to those depicted in Hollywood blockbusters.

Science emphasizes empirical evidence, but just as people cannot prove geological changes like the shifting of seas and continents in a laboratory—on a scale far beyond what humans can simulate in terms of time and space—the same issue applies to climate change assessments. Humans should always maintain humility regarding their cognitive abilities, as there are many aspects in which we neither fully understand the world nor recognize our own limitations. Scientific research can only say that, based on long-term climate data comparisons, there is a significant correlation between temperature and carbon dioxide levels. However, this became a reason for Trump to dismiss climate change policies, arguing that since climate change is not man-made and other variables exist, this correlation is merely speculative and cannot serve as a basis for policy-making. Nevertheless, the vast majority of scientists believe that human activities, especially carbon dioxide emissions, are indeed the primary cause of climate change and can be quantitatively calculated.

The Intergovernmental Panel on Climate Change (IPCC) assessment concludes that the global climate is indeed warming, primarily due to human activities such as burning fossil fuels and deforestation, which release large amounts of greenhouse gases into the atmosphere, exacerbating the greenhouse effect. Data from the World Meteorological Organization indicate that 2015, 2016, 2017, and 2018 were confirmed as the four warmest years since records began in 1850, with the 20 warmest years on record all occurring in the past 22 years. According to a report from the U.S. National Oceanic and Atmospheric Administration (NOAA), the global average concentration of carbon dioxide in the atmosphere has risen from around 280 ppm (parts per million) before the Industrial

Revolution to 389 ppm in 2010, reaching an official figure of 405.5 ppm in 2018 and setting a new record of 415.26 ppm in May 2019.

Humans have engaged in prolonged discussions on addressing climate change. Since the birth of the *United Nations Framework Convention on Climate Change* in 1992, countries have conducted a series of negotiations on climate change response. Initially intended to address climate warming, these negotiations have increasingly become a platform for countries to vie for interests and influence.

In December 2015, the United Nations Climate Conference was held in Paris, where countries reached a landmark agreement known as *the Paris Agreement*. The agreement sets a clear core goal for controlling climate change: limiting the global temperature increase to well below 2°C above pre-industrial levels and pursuing efforts to limit the temperature increase to 1.5°C.

The greatest contribution of *the Paris Agreement* lies in defining a clear "hard target" for global pursuit. Only by achieving a global peak in greenhouse gas emissions as soon as possible and reaching net-zero greenhouse gas emissions in the second half of the 21st century can we reduce the ecological risks posed by climate change to the Earth and the survival crisis faced by humanity.

The Paris Agreement incorporates all countries worldwide into a community of shared future for protecting the Earth's ecology and safeguarding human development, transcending the narrow mindset of "zero-sum games" and reflecting a strong desire among participants for more sharing, more responsibility, and mutual benefit and win-win outcomes.

The Paris Agreement also provides a compass for the direction of economic and energy development. Economy and energy are closely intertwined, and Jeremy Rifkin's description of the Third Industrial Revolution four years ago has found strong resonance. *The Paris Agreement* encourages all parties to participate in global climate change response actions through "nationally determined contributions" and actively transition to green and sustainable growth models, which will undoubtedly have a significant impact on the development of related industries. It also calls for developed countries to continue taking the lead in emission reductions and strengthening financial support for developing countries, enhancing technological development and technology transfer cooperation, with far-reaching implications for the content of international cooperation. In line with *the Paris Agreement's* initiatives, it will also influence capital markets, guiding global investment to further tilt towards green energy, low-carbon economies, and environmental governance.

The impact of *the Paris Agreement* on the energy sector is the most direct and profound. The primary source of greenhouse gas emissions is fossil fuels. The combustion of carbon-rich fossil fuels, in addition to obtaining energy, primarily produces carbon dioxide as a byproduct.

Since the Industrial Revolution, carbon dioxide emissions related to energy have been on the rise, except for individual years of economic crises. This growth curve paused slightly for three years after 2014, but before we could catch our breath, energy-related carbon dioxide emissions began to rise again from 2017, reaching a new high in 2018 (Figure 1-5).

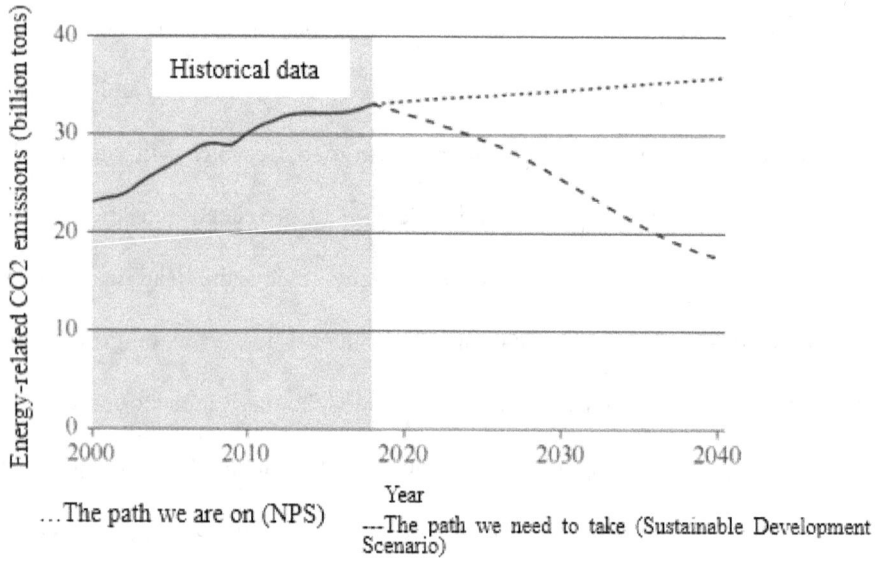

Figure 1-5 Energy-related Carbon Dioxide Emissions and Outlook

(Source: IEA)

According to the International Energy Agency's outlook, if the temperature control goals of *the Paris Agreement* are to be achieved, the carbon dioxide emission curve in the energy sector should follow the lower line, whereas under current policy scenarios, it would follow the upper line, highlighting the immense pressure faced by energy development.

Since the onset of industrialization, we have emitted 2.2 trillion tons of carbon dioxide equivalent (including other greenhouse gases converted) into the atmosphere. To maintain the goal of limiting global warming to no more than 2°C and avoid more severe chain reactions, we should control additional emissions to no more than 700 billion tons. The time left to solve this problem is already very limited. Currently, we emit approximately 42 billion tons annually, with 33 billion tons coming from energy-related emissions. At this rate, even if annual emissions do not increase, we will reach the emission limit in just 17 years.

People eagerly hope for a gradual reduction in emissions, with some European countries explicitly proposing a zero-emission vision by 2050. However, in reality, energy-related carbon dioxide emissions, after three years of stability, significantly increased again in 2018.

To curb the growth of energy-related carbon dioxide emissions, countries worldwide are taking various measures, such as improving energy efficiency, restricting the construction of new inefficient coal-fired power plants, phasing out old and inefficient coal-fired power plants, prompting the oil and gas industry to reduce direct methane emissions, and accelerating the reduction of fossil fuel subsidies. Europe established a carbon market in 2005, hoping to reduce carbon dioxide emissions through market-based mechanisms. Despite ongoing controversies, it has played an irreplaceable role, primarily by making the industry recognize that emission reductions have become a routine consideration. After years of preparation and pilot programs, the Chinese government announced in 2017 that it would officially establish a carbon emissions market in 2020, starting with the power generation sector, which has the largest emission volume.

Even though the United States, under President Trump's leadership, withdrew from *the Paris Agreement*, the country has not halted its emission reduction efforts. California, New York, and Washington quickly formed the "United States Climate Alliance," continuing to vigorously promote their clean energy transition plans and calling on more businesses to continue their emission reduction efforts in line with *the Paris Agreement*. Market forces are stronger than individuals, and thanks to the success of the shale gas revolution, natural gas in the United States is very cheap, leading to a large-scale replacement of coal with natural gas for power generation, coupled with the rapid development of renewable energy and improved energy efficiency. As a result, carbon emissions in the United States continued to decline after withdrawing from *the Paris Agreement* until they rose in tandem with the global trend in 2018. Some scholars believe that climate change may still be a flag that the United States will raise again in the post-Trump era, as it is also one of the most important means of regulating global economic development.

In September 2018, California Governor Jerry Brown signed a bill proposing that by 2045, California will achieve a 100% clean energy supply for electricity, completely abandoning traditional fossil fuel power generation methods such as coal.

In May 2019, data from the UK's National Grid showed that the country achieved a record 114 consecutive hours without coal-fired power generation since the Industrial Revolution. Spokesperson Sean Kemp said, "The trend of renewable energy replacing coal-fired power generation has been established." The UK government plans to close its last coal-fired power plants by 2025 to reduce carbon emissions. In recent years, the proportion of coal-fired power generation in the UK's total power generation has continuously declined, currently accounting for less than 10%. As of early May 2019, coal consumption has decreased by nearly two-thirds compared to the same period last year, with a total of over 1,000 hours of coal-free power generation. In 2019, it will easily surpass the 2018 record of 1,800 hours of coal-free power generation. Meanwhile, the proportion of renewable energy power generation has been increasing in recent years, with wind power generation exceeding 150 billion kilowatt-hours for the first time in 2018.

Traditional energy projects have long lifecycles, taking several years from planning to implementation and often operating for more than 20 years, with nuclear power plants lasting 30 to 40 years or even longer.

Therefore, without a forward-looking perspective, many of our investments may face increasingly difficult futures from the outset and may even become stranded assets. As the pressure to reduce emissions continues to increase, policy environments may be vastly different in ten years, and project boundary conditions will inevitably change significantly. These are issues that must be considered and addressed now.

The Campaign to Defend the Blue Sky

While the international community, or developed countries, may focus more on carbon dioxide emissions, developing countries are more concerned with air pollution—a sentiment deeply felt by the Chinese people. In fact, air pollution remains a global issue, and many cities in India experience worse air quailty than cities in China. Even in numerous European cities, air pollution is a significant concern; Paris, for instance, has implemented tiered vehicle management due to air pollution in the past few years, restricting traffic during severe pollution episodes. In Africa, although industrial pollution is minimal, the use of traditional energy sources like firewood indoors causes severe indoor pollution.

Air pollution primarily includes particulate matter (PM), ozone (O3), nitrogen dioxide (NO2), and sulfur dioxide (SO2), posing a major environmental risk to health and leading to various diseases such as respiratory infections, heart disease, and lung cancer. The United Nations estimates that outdoor air pollution causes 1.3 million deaths worldwide annually, while indoor air pollution results in approximately 2 million premature deaths, with about half of these being children under five years old dying from pneumonia.

Urban air pollution in Asia is among the worst globally. According to UN statistics, 12 of the world's top 15 cities with the highest levels of particulate pollution are in Asia. Moreover, six of these 12 cities also have high concentrations of atmospheric SO2, with air pollution levels significantly exceeding the international air quality guidelines recommended by the World Health Organization (WHO).

On Wikipedia, the smog event in Beijing during the winter of 2015-2016 has become an entry. Since then, "iron-fisted" measures to combat smog have become the norm. Many people vividly remember that event, during which unconventional methods were employed, albeit with limited short-term effects.

The desire for blue skies has become universal, leading to humorous terms like "Parade Blue" and "Two Sessions Blue," implicitly conveying the message that people are willing to slow down development for cleaner air. The question, "What is the purpose of our development?" has never been more tangible.

Subsequent years have witnessed unprecedented efforts to combat smog. In response to persistently high levels of winter air pollution, the Beijing-Tianjin-Hebei region implemented staggered production strategies at the end of 2016, requiring cement, foundry, and some steel enterprises in multiple cities to halt production from November to March the following year. This clearly signaled that economic development should not come at the expense of the environment.

Under this philosophy, relevant central ministries, along with six provinces and municipalities—Beijing, Tianjin, Hebei, Shanxi, Shandong, and Henan—established the Beijing-Tianjin-Hebei Air Pollution Control Zone. In addition to Beijing and Tianjin, this zone includes 26 cities, collectively known as "2+26." In this area, stricter air pollution prevention and control policies will be enforced, prioritizing ecological conservation over economic gains. Subsequently, the experience of the Beijing-Tianjin-Hebei region was extended to the Yangtze River Delta and Pearl River Delta regions, where environmental capacities are also nearing their limits despite their economic prosperity.

The 2016 Energy Work Guidance issued by the National Energy Administration explicitly stated that no new coal-fired power generation capacity would be planned in key areas for air pollution prevention, and several planned or approved (under construction) coal-fired power projects would be canceled, postponed for review, or construction suspended. Environmental protection has become the most crucial constraint on energy development.

Figure 1-6 shows the changes in atmospheric particulate matter levels and natural gas consumption in the "2+26" cities as statistically analyzed by the IEA. To control air pollution, the northern regions have widely promoted the switch from coal to natural gas. Clean energy is directly linked to improved air quality, with particulate matter levels continuously decreasing as natural gas consumption rises in these areas.

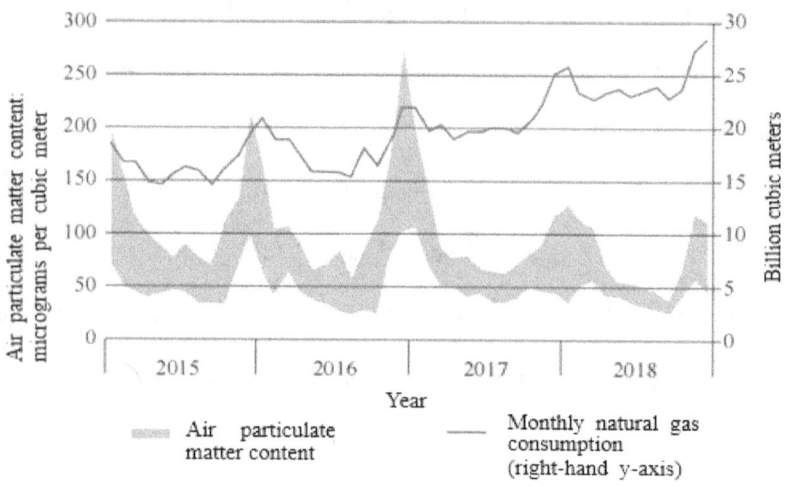

Figure 1-6 Growth in Natural Gas Consumption and Reduction in

Pollution in the Beijing-Tianjin-Hebei Region (Source: IEA)

The results have been remarkable. According to a report titled *A Review of 20 Years' Air Pollution Control in Beijing* released by the United Nations Environment Programme in early 2019, Beijing's annual average PM2.5 concentration in 2018 was 51, showing significant improvement. However, this figure is still notably higher than China's current national standard and the WHO's minimum guideline of 35. The average PM2.5 level in major cities across the 28 EU countries is below 15, while in major U.S. cities, it is less than 10. From this perspective, the road to smog control is still long, and many restrictive policies in the energy sector will become the "new normal."

The report of the 19th National Congress of the Communist Party of China incorporated the concept of "lucid waters and lush mountains are invaluable assets" into party and government documents, elevating the fight against air pollution to the level of an environmental protection campaign. It called for "persistent efforts to prevent and control air pollution through joint governance by all members of society and prevention at the source, aiming to win the Campaign to Defend the Blue Sky." This campaign has become a resounding slogan, with former Premier Li Keqiang specifically requesting the use of premier funds to investigate the causes of smog for targeted treatment.

During the 2018 Two Sessions, the Ministry of Environmental Protection released research findings compiled by over 2,000 experts over two years, attributing smog formation to the environmental capacity in the Beijing-Tianjin-Hebei region reaching its limit. Although this may seem like common sense, it faced criticism online. Nevertheless, from an administrative standpoint, it is a highly actionable conclusion. Reaching the limit means that even a small increase in pollution sources could lead to severe consequences, making it self-evident that new pollution sources should be strictly restricted, with fossil energy projects being the primary target. As mentioned earlier, the approval of new coal-fired power plants in the Beijing-Tianjin-Hebei region was halted two years ago. For traditional energy enterprises, this transition from double-digit annual growth to restricted approvals is undoubtedly challenging and painful.

In fact, as early as 2013, the Chinese government proposed the concept of controlling total energy consumption. In early that year, the State Council issued the 12*th Five-Year Plan for Energy Development*, requiring the implementation of "dual control" over total energy consumption and intensity by 2015, with the national total energy consumption and electricity consumption capped at 4 billion tons of standard coal equivalent and 6.15 trillion kilowatt-hours, respectively. It also aimed to reduce energy consumption per unit of GDP by 16% from 2010 levels and improve overall energy efficiency to 38%.

When these control policies were established, resource constraints were likely the primary consideration, influenced by long-standing theories like "peak oil," which suggested that finite oil resources would eventually reach production limits, leading to resource panic. However, technological advancements, particularly the large-scale development of shale oil and gas in the United States and the significant reduction in new energy costs, have fundamentally alleviated resource constraints. Resource limitations are no longer an imminent issue, with the environment becoming the most significant external factor in energy development.

New Energy Business Models

The internet era has brought about the most profound change in the mode of information flow, shifting from a pyramid-shaped information collection and dissemination model to a completely flattened one. In the past, only traditional media outlets like radio stations and newspapers had the power to disseminate information, making access to information a privilege for a select few. However, the internet initially disrupted this ecosystem, enabling everyone to become a news agency. In the process of sharing information, its value does not diminish but rather increases. One could say that everyone has become both a producer and a consumer of information—a "prosumer." Through platforms like WeChat, Weibo, Douyin (or Facebook and YouTube overseas), we have transformed from passive readers into content providers. The internet has empowered everyone to become frontline reporters, profoundly altering our media landscape. Some internet celebrities have even surpassed TV hosts in popularity.

In the energy sector, since the advent of modern society, there has been a clear divide between energy providers and consumers. Energy providers, primarily large enterprises, have occupied the top of the pyramid, enjoying a certain degree of monopoly. Despite continuous advancements in various energy technologies, the fundamental model of obtaining electricity from the grid, heating from heating companies, and natural gas from gas companies has remained largely unchanged for over a century.

However, the situation is changing. Energy prosumers are emerging rapidly, indicating a clear trend that promises revolutionary changes in the energy supply methods for households and communities.

This shift in the energy model stems from the rapid development of renewable energy sources such as photovoltaic and wind power, the proliferation of home energy storage systems and electric vehicles, and the increasingly flexible interconnection capabilities of smart grids. These factors have enabled residential and industrial customers, traditionally energy consumers, to also become energy producers (Figure 1-7).

Figure 1-7 Comparison between Traditional Energy Consumers and

Energy Prosumers

(Chart by Sarah Harman from the U.S. Department of Energy website)

Who can become energy prosumers? The answer is: an increasing number of people. Roof-mounted PV panels, backyard wind turbines, geothermal energy, biogas, energy storage devices—these are all common local energy resources. Electric vehicles themselves also serve as mobile energy storage stations. Not only households but also factories, hospitals, shopping malls, communities, and even cities can become energy prosumers.

Both domestically and internationally, with the rapid decline in the costs of renewable energy and energy storage, more and more people are leveraging local, decentralized energy resources to meet their own energy needs. Roof-mounted PV panels are the most widely adopted application. The era of one-way electricity consumption is fading, and smart grids are blurring the lines between electricity generation and consumption.

In 2015, *People's Daily* reported on the "PV Pension" initiative in Ganglingxia Village, Jinhua, Zhejiang Province. Villager Jiang Hongxing receives over 300 yuan ($45) in "pension" each month from the bank in town, which comes from the income generated by selling electricity from his PV power station connected to the grid and policy subsidies provided by State Grid Zhejiang Jinhua Power Supply Company. The PV power station has become Jiang's primary source of income. "I'll rely on the roof-mounted power station for my pension in the future. With over 300 yuan per month, plus the rural social insurance for my wife and me, we'll have enough to live on," he said.

Jiang Hongliang, the first villager to install roof-mounted PV panels and the village party secretary, calculated the costs and benefits: "I installed 3 kilowatts of solar PV panels, investing a total of 18,000 yuan after village subsidies. On average, I generate about 300 kilowatt-hours of electricity per month. With the electricity tariff and subsidies, I earn 1 yuan per kilowatt-hour, totaling 3,600 yuan annually." He said that given the relatively low cost of living in rural areas, choosing PV for pension is quite ideal, with an investment return rate of about 20% and a payback period of 30 years, allowing him to recoup his investment in about six years. In recent years, the "PV Pension" initiative has seen explosive growth in rural Zhejiang.

According to reports, to provide better supporting services, Jinhua City has explored three models tailored to farmers' needs:

Owner Model: Conditionally well-off farmers can purchase PV systems outright, recovering their investment in 5-7 years with an average annual return of 12%-20% on their investment.

"PV Loan" Model: Through cooperation with banks, farmers can obtain a "PV loan" with a 30% down payment and a 3-year installment plan, allowing them to enjoy the benefits of the PV power station immediately while making manageable repayments.

Leasing Model: Farmers can lease their roofs to PV companies, which invest in and construct PV power stations using a full feed-in tariff model. The PV companies and residents share the revenue from selling electricity, enabling low-income farmers with limited financial capacity to achieve PV pensions by renting out their idle roofs. Residents can choose among these three models based on their actual situations and needs, fully enjoying national and provincial subsidies, electricity generation revenue, and savings on electricity bills.

Similar stories have unfolded elsewhere in the world. In Wadebridge, a town in the UK, Steve Kessell, who runs a bed-and-breakfast, installed PV panels on his roof in 2014, taking advantage of government subsidies at the time. Steve calculated that he saves 1,800 pounds annually on his electricity bills, allowing him to recoup his initial investment in six years. In other parts of the UK with less favorable sunlight, it might take 10 years or more to recover the investment. Steve is pleased with his decision, as the money saved is equivalent to money earned.

This project is not without its imperfections, as it lacks energy storage facilities. Steve's strategy is to perform high-energy-consuming tasks like laundry, baking, and ironing during the day when the PV panels are generating electricity. Considering that PV costs have more than halved over the past five years and energy storage has become more affordable, Steve would achieve even better results today, even without subsidies.

Indeed, the development of roof-mounted PV in Europe has faced some criticism, as those with large roofs tend to be wealthier individuals, leading to accusations that subsidies inadvertently support the rich at the expense of the poor. However, these pioneers have demonstrated the potential of PV, and thanks to government subsidies, the PV industry has achieved rapid breakthroughs, accelerating its transition to a subsidy-free stage.

The following figure illustrates the development trend of distributed PV (primarily for households and businesses) in China. The growth rate of distributed PV has surpassed that of centralized PV (Figure 1-8). This figure is based on actual data from 2016 and predicts that by 2018, the actual installed capacity will significantly exceed projections, with the main growth coming from distributed PV installations. This also indicates that the pace of real-world development has far outstripped predictions.

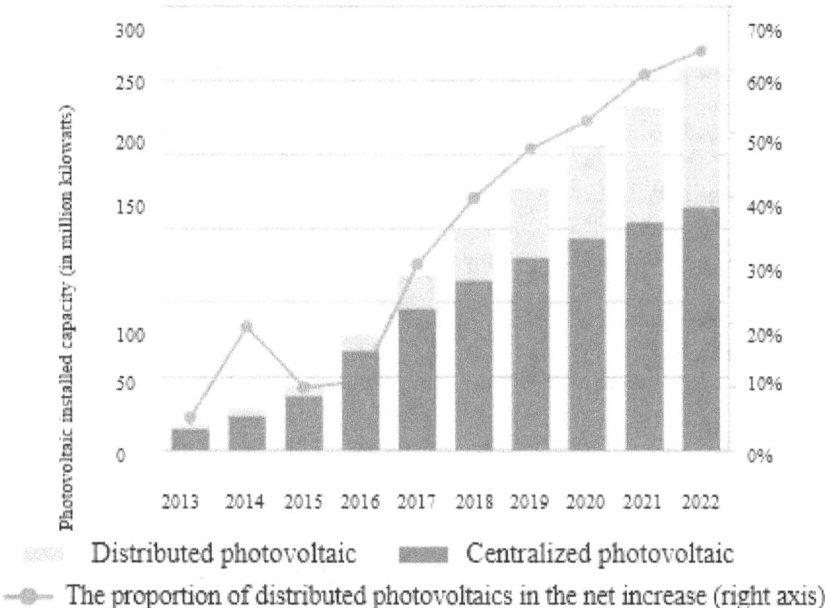

Figure 1-8 Cumulative Installed Capacity and Forecast of Distributed and Centralized Photovoltaic Power in China (Source: IEA, 2017)

In 2018, China added 44 million kilowatts of PV capacity, bringing the cumulative installed capacity to 174 million kilowatts, ranking first globally and surpassing the entire power capacity of France. According to data from the China Photovoltaic Industry Association, in 2018, newly added centralized PV capacity was 20.8 million kilowatts, while distributed PV capacity reached 23.2 million kilowatts, accounting for 52.7% and surpassing centralized PV for the first time. In 2019, this trend continued, with small-scale residential distributed PV accounting for nearly half of the new installations.

For large-scale industrial and commercial users, energy prosumers have access to a wider range of options, including natural gas-based combined cooling, heating, and power (CCHP) systems. Shanghai Disneyland serves as a prime example. Covering 116 hectares with hundreds of buildings, Shanghai Disneyland is the first Disney park worldwide to adopt a distributed energy system. The park's energy supply system can centrally provide four types of energy: cooling, heating, electricity, and compressed air (for amusement facilities). By achieving energy cascade utilization (i.e., using waste heat from power generation for heating or cooling), the overall primary energy utilization rate exceeds 85%, nearly doubling the energy efficiency compared to conventional methods. The project utilizes natural gas as its primary energy source and plans to use ten 4.4-megawatt internal combustion engines. In addition to using waste heat for refrigeration, heating, and steam generation, the system can also store cold and heat in water for peak shaving. The project has operated smoothly since its commissioning, yielding good economic returns.

Of course, such an energy supply system requires a more intelligent "brain." The project employs an intelligent optimization control system that more accurately matches energy production with demand. Through temperature sensors, pressure sensors, and ultrasonic flowmeters, the system monitors parameters such as water temperature and pressure in the piping network in real-time. The centralized control system optimizes and coordinates operations in real-time, responding promptly to the park's energy demands. Additionally, through big data analysis, the system can predict the park's energy needs in advance and provide optimal economic operating plans for major equipment, achieving the best match between energy production and demand.

Biomass energy is another highly suitable option for localized utilization. Often overlooked, biomass energy accounted for approximately 3% of global primary energy consumption (excluding firewood and bioethanol) in 2018. Unlike other renewable energy sources like wind and solar, which do not cause environmental harm if left unused, many types of biomass require proper disposal; otherwise, they can lead to environmental pollution. In China, preventing the open burning of straw to avoid air pollution has become a significant headache for local governments at all levels. However, if straw is left untreated, it can hinder farming and reduce land productivity due to degradation. Given the low energy density of biomass, long-distance transportation is often uneconomical, making localized utilization the optimal choice. Thus, distributed biomass energy utilization offers both economic and social benefits.

The following figure shows the distribution of biomass projects across Germany, densely populated with numerous small-scale initiatives. This includes nearly 10,000 biomass gas projects, most of which are distributed and typical examples of energy prosumers (Figure 1-9).

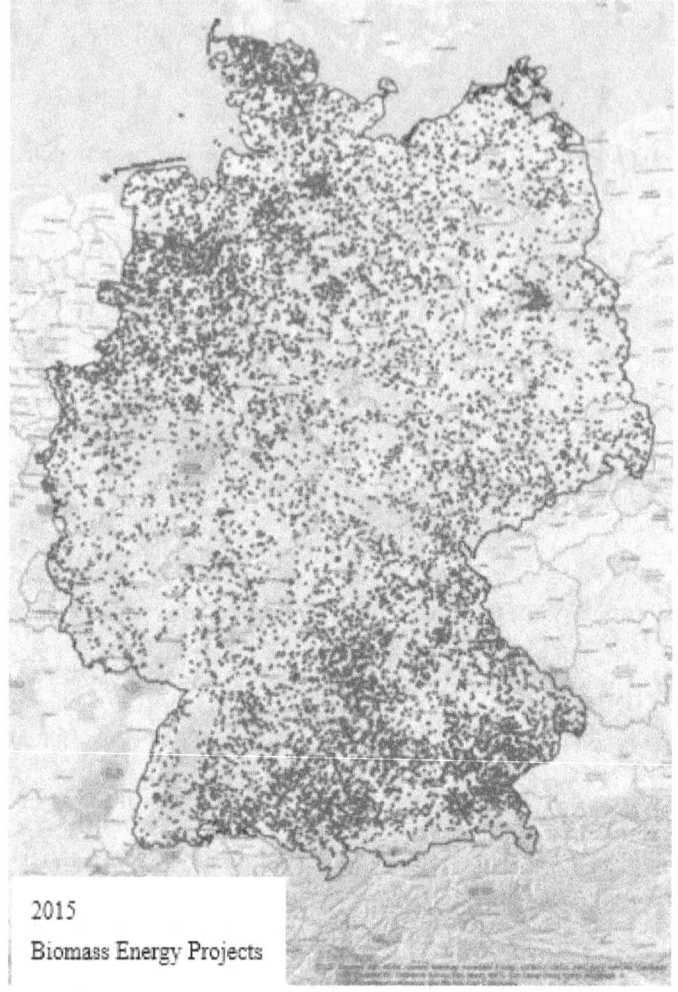

Figure 1-9 Schematic Diagram of the Distribution of Biomass Energy

Projects in Germany (Source: Data, 2019)

Notably, biomass gas (Biogas) is highly developed in Germany. Agricultural waste is fermented in specialized digesters, producing methane and other gases that can be used directly for low-heat-value power generation or further purified and injected into the natural gas grid. This has become a mature industry, with Germany's largest gas company, Uniper, also developing many biogas projects.

The rise of energy prosumers hinges on the supporting infrastructure provided by smart grids, which can flexibly accommodate distributed electricity generation (Figure 1-10) and provide the necessary support; otherwise, they would remain isolated energy islands. Governments worldwide have recognized the opportunities presented by energy prosumers and have introduced policies to support their development. The U.S. Department of Energy launched the Grid Modernization Initiative (GMI) to promote energy prosumers by accelerating smart grid construction. GMI provides substantial support for advanced energy storage technologies, clean energy grid integration, and other related grid modernization research and development. The initiative focuses on future grid architecture concepts, tools, and technologies, enabling measurement, analysis, prediction, and protection of future grid characteristics, thereby facilitating broader adoption of these technologies and tools.

1990   **2014**

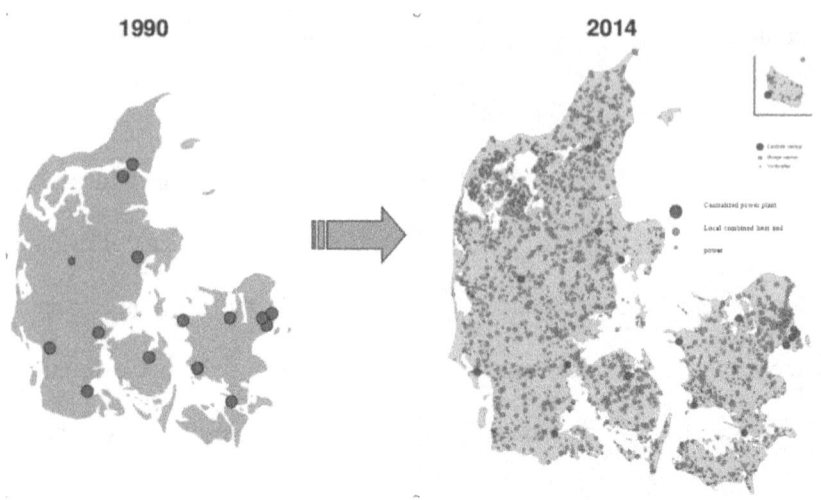

Figure 1-10 Comparison of Denmark's energy development: The

development of distributed energy has made energy supply cleaner,

cheaper, and more reliable (Source: David Roberts)

China is also vigorously promoting smart grid construction. In 2017, the National Energy Administration launched a batch of smart energy and multi-energy complementary demonstration projects. Although this field is still in its infancy, many projects already exhibit characteristics of regional energy prosumers in their design. These projects not only test and explore better technologies and business models but also provide valuable insights for policy adjustments.

With the acceleration of global urbanization, the pressure on building energy consumption in cities will continue to grow. Urban regional energy systems, which integrate various new energy sources ("source expansion") while utilizing waste heat and improving energy efficiency ("conservation"), will play an increasingly important role. A 2015 report by the United Nations Environment Programme, *District Energy in Cities: Unlocking the Potential of Energy Efficiency and Renewable Energy*, analyzed best practices in 48 cities worldwide from technical, policy, and financing perspectives. The findings are encouraging: if cities globally adopt efficient, green, and safe regional energy systems, they could contribute up to 50% of global energy savings and 59% of emission reductions needed to achieve the 2030 Sustainable Development Goals.

The rise of energy prosumers points to an exciting trend that represents one of the optimal directions for renewable energy application. By eliminating the need for long-distance transportation, efficiency is significantly enhanced, and investment costs are reduced, benefiting the environment while creating new economic growth points. In terms of energy security, distributed energy systems are less susceptible to large-scale grid outages and can even provide "black start" support to the grid. Moreover, energy consumption will shed its traditionally industrial-heavy image and take on a more personalized and "cool" character. Green energy will no longer be the exclusive domain of large corporations. While star companies like Google and L'Oréal have announced achieving 100% green energy for their products, households and individuals can also economically achieve high proportions of green energy consumption, reflecting their personal preferences. Of course, this process involves business model innovation, with the core issue being who will cover the additional costs. However, as the costs of green energy decrease and energy service efficiency improves, this gap is rapidly narrowing.

The rise of energy prosumers enables energy to become a means for consumers to express their values and aspirations, much like growing their preferred vegetables in their backyard. Bertrand Piccard, the first person to circumnavigate the globe in a solar-powered aircraft, has frequently shared his insights with me during conversations and speeches. He once said, "Our greatest challenge in today's world is not to conquer space but to live a high-quality life." This statement left a deep impression on me. He also said, "My solar-powered aircraft may not carry a single passenger, but it carries an important message: we can achieve global circumnavigation without fossil fuels. Humans need to change not the world but our own mindsets."

Leaders in New Energy

The term "leader" is full of promise. To accelerate the progress of China's photovoltaic (PV) power generation technology, promote industrial upgrading, drive down the cost of PV power generation, reduce electricity prices, decrease subsidies, and ultimately achieve grid parity, the National Energy Administration, together with relevant departments, proposed the implementation of the PV Power Generation "Leader" Program and the construction of leader bases in 2015. The bidding results of the third batch of leader projects revealed that the bids in some regions had already fallen below the local thermal power prices, indicating that PV power was ushering in the era of grid parity.

Each year, the China Renewable Energy Engineering Institute releases the *China Renewable Energy Development Report*. According to the latest report, in 2018, the average construction cost of onshore wind power projects in China further decreased compared to 2017, with an average cost per kilowatt of approximately 7,100 yuan. In some regions, the cost per kilowatt of wind power projects had dropped below 6,000 yuan. The installed capacity of PV power generation continued to expand, with an average cost per kilowatt of about 5,500 yuan for the whole year, a year-on-year decrease of 15%. The cost per kilowatt of some PV power plants had even fallen below 5,000 yuan. Grid parity for PV power had been achieved in multiple regions.

PV power is the fastest-growing and most tumultuous industry within the renewable energy sector. It has given rise to numerous rapidly emerging enterprises and has also witnessed the bursting of countless bubbles amid fierce competition and policy changes. However, there is no denying that over the past decade, the average cost of PV power has decreased by around 80%. Besides the cost reductions brought about by economies of scale, the key factor has been technological progress, with continuous improvements in photoelectric conversion efficiency. Only one industry can match such a significant cost reduction—the information technology industry, namely the digital and internet sectors. This also foreshadows an increasingly close integration between the PV and information industries in the future, which will further drive a major industrial revolution.

In May 2019, Noor Abu Dhabi, the world's largest single solar PV power plant, was connected to the grid in Abu Dhabi. This 1,177-MW PV power plant had set multiple world records, not only being the largest of its kind but also achieving the lowest price through competitive bidding. In 2016, a consortium consisting of Japan's Marubeni and China's JinkoSolar won the bid with a price of 2.42 U.S. cents/kWh, equivalent to less than 0.15 yuan per kilowatt-hour in Chinese currency, which was already far lower than the feed-in tariffs of many thermal power plants (Figure 1-11).

Figure 1-11 Aerial View of the 1,000 MW Photovoltaic Base in Abu

Dhabi (Source: Newatlas)

The desert regions in the Middle East enjoy intense sunlight, with annual solar radiation nearly double that of temperate regions. In these areas, land is cheap or even free, coupled with favorable fiscal and tax policies and low financing costs, and all of these contribute to the realization of low electricity prices. Of course, the progress and cost reductions in PV technology have been the most crucial driving forces. Traditional fossil fuel-producing countries in the Middle East and North Africa have high hopes for the development of new energy and aim to reduce their dependence on oil through new energy advancements. An additional incentive is that new energy power generation consumes minimal water resources, a critical factor in these arid regions where water is extremely scarce.

The record for low electricity prices in Abu Dhabi did not last long. Subsequently, in 2017, Mexico's Ministry of Energy launched a multi-megawatt PV procurement bidding process, and Italy's ENEL Green Power offered a bid of 1.77 US cents/kWh (equivalent to approximately 0.12 yuan/kWh in Chinese currency), exceeding many people's expectations.

Over the past decade or so, China's PV module manufacturing industry has seen both successes and failures, with many enterprises experiencing significant ups and downs. However, the industry's overall output has maintained rapid and sustained growth. The customer base has shifted from being predominantly export-oriented to a balanced split between international and domestic markets.

According to data from the China Photovoltaic Industry Association, in 2018, China's national PV module output reached 85.7 gigawatts, a year-on-year increase of 14.3%. It is expected to exceed 90 gigawatts in 2019 (Figure 1-12), with roughly half of this output being exported to international markets. China manufactures over 70% of the world's PV modules and is both the largest producer and installer of PV equipment globally, serving as an undeniable leader in the field (Figure 1-13). Besides the industry's efforts, the continuous support from the Chinese government over the years has also played a crucial role. When new technologies first emerge, government support often enables a country's industrial scale to expand rapidly, gaining international competitiveness and widening the gap with followers. This is why, despite accusations of non-market economy behavior, countries still provide various forms of support and even subsidies. However, this approach is somewhat similar to venture capital, with a high risk of most investments going to waste, and China has numerous examples of such outcomes.

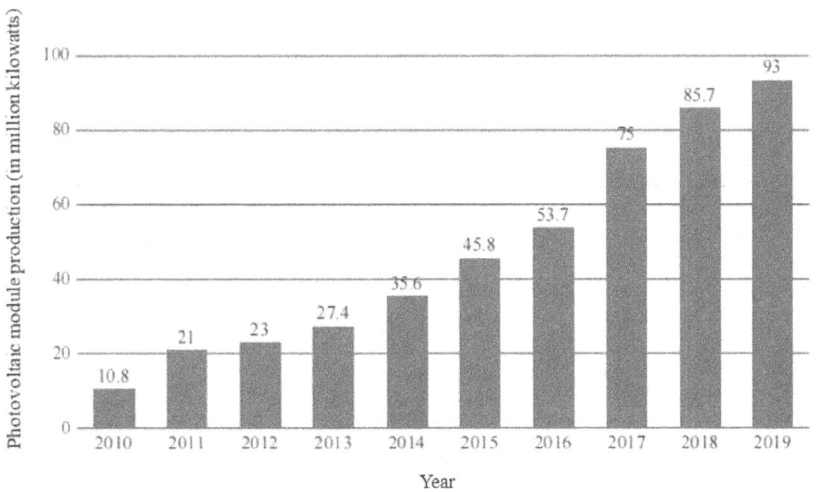

Figure 1-12 Production Volume of Photovoltaic Modules in China from 2010 to 2019 (Source: China Photovoltaic Industry Association)

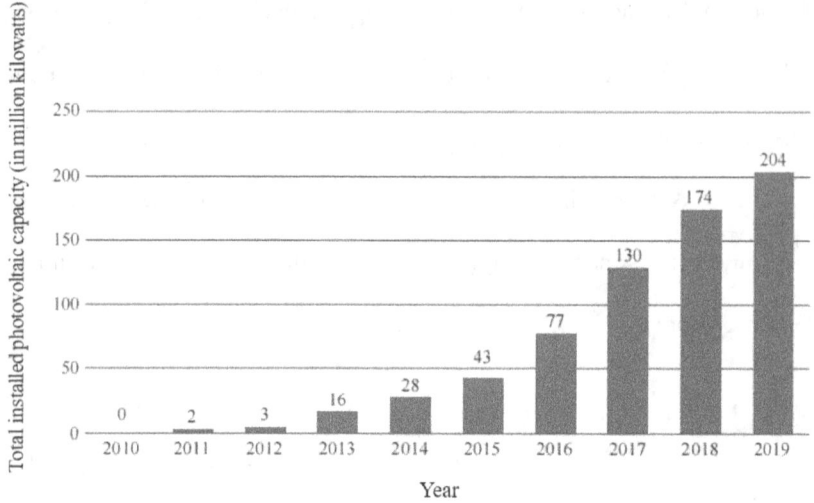

Figure 1-13 Growth Trend of Total Installed Photovoltaic Capacity in

China (Source: China Photovoltaic Industry Association)

In September 2017, the first dedicated PV museum opened in Yangzhong, Jiangsu Province (Figure 1-14). Dr. Shi Zhengrong, who once became China's richest man through the PV industry, attended the opening ceremony in his hometown. His past glory seemed to be a thing of the past as he enthusiastically discussed the personalized applications of PV power.

This museum is claimed to be China's first PV expo. Behind it lies a large cluster of PV and related industry enterprises that have developed in the Yangzhong area. Such industrial clusters exist in many cities across China and have become important engines for local economic development.

Right outside the museum, in a pond, several PV aerators were in operation, with PV-powered motors driving the blades to aerate the water.

Such direct applications eliminate the need for power transmission, resulting in higher efficiency. The PV industry in Yangzhong has developed into a cluster, with the number of enterprises in the PV industrial park continuously increasing. While competition prompts enterprises to continuously improve their technological levels and reduce costs, it also stimulates them to create more personalized applications, such as colored tile-style PV roofs, seeking new growth points for the PV industry through personalized designs.

Figure 1-14 China Photovoltaic Museum

(Photo Source: Yangzhong Municipal Government)

A decade ago, people could not have imagined that the cost of this industry would decrease so rapidly, let alone that PV power generation could compete on an equal footing with conventional power plants in terms of cost. Now, this is becoming a reality. Based on this trend, the

International Energy Agency's World Energy Outlook 2018 report declared that in the next decade, in different regions worldwide (considering factors such as solar resources and cost conditions), PV power will become the cheapest form of power generation in terms of comprehensive costs at different times (Figure 1-15). In other words, in the future, people will flock to PV products not only because they are green and zero-carbon but also because they represent the cheapest way to generate electricity.

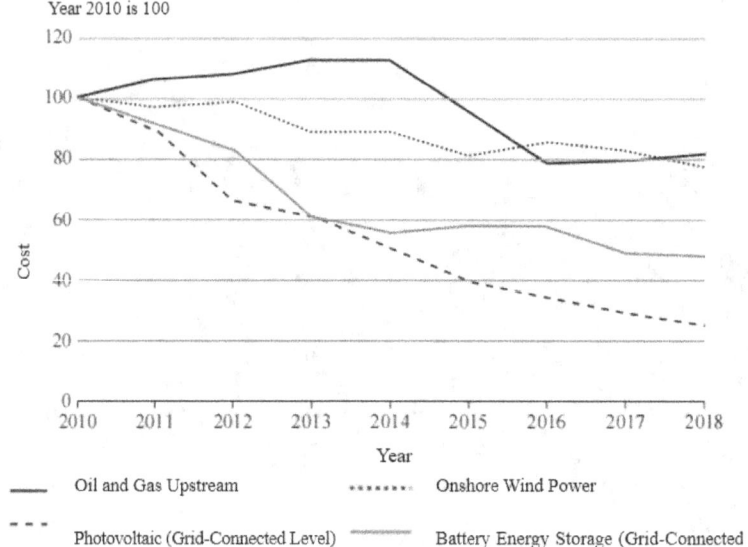

Figure 1-15 Capital Costs of Different Energy Sources and Fuels

(Source: IRENA)

Mobile Energy Storage Stations

Electricity is produced and consumed simultaneously, and power storage facilities are required when production and consumption do not match. Peak shaving and energy storage are essential in the power system for ensuring the safe and stable operation. In energy systems with increasing variable photovoltaic and wind power, the importance of energy storage continues to grow.

Among traditional energy storage methods, pumped hydro storage is the most significant, with a global installed capacity of approximately 150 million kilowatts. Water is pumped from a downstream reservoir to an upper reservoir on a mountain during periods of low electricity demand. Then, during peak demand periods, the water is released to generate electricity, meeting the grid's need for peak shaving and valley filling. Pumped hydro storage power stations are often located in scenic areas with mountains and water. However, this also becomes a limiting factor. On one hand, such locations are not ubiquitous; on the other hand, not all of them are suitable for development.

In recent years, with technological advancements, battery energy storage has experienced rapid growth, with the capacity of newly installed capacity increasing year by year, approaching the new installed capacity of pumped hydro storage. Compared to pumped hydro storage, battery energy storage offers greater flexibility in terms of scale and installation location. It can serve the grid as a centralized power station or be used as a household energy storage product.

By the end of 2018, the cumulative installed capacity of battery energy storage worldwide had exceeded 8 million kilowatts. The amount of newly installed battery energy storage in 2018 nearly doubled compared to that in 2017 (Figure 1-16). In particular, the growth of newly installed battery energy storage on the user side has been rapid, with the new installation volume nearly tripling that of 2017. The main countries driving this growth are South Korea, followed by China, the United States, and Germany. Emerging markets, including Southeast Asia and South Africa, are also developing rapidly, largely thanks to strong policy support for electric vehicles. This rapid development has also benefited from a rapid decline in costs. For example, from 2016 to 2017, the price per unit of battery decreased by 22%.

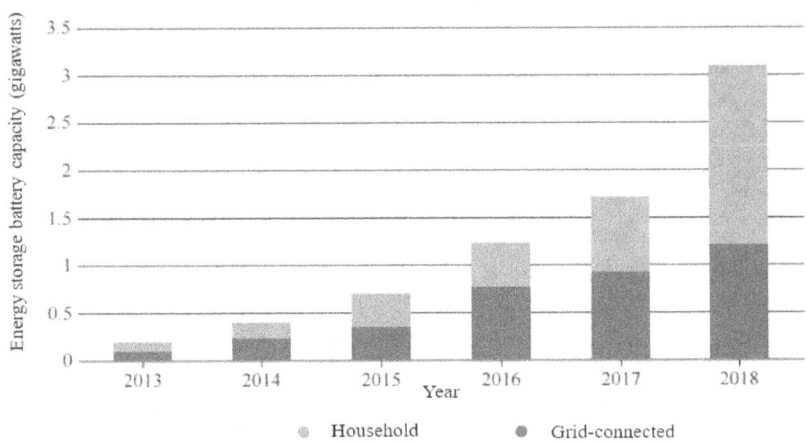

Figure 1-16 Energy Storage Battery Capacity Commissioned from 2013

to 2018 (Source: IEA)

Energy storage can also be seen as a significant opportunity in the new energy sector. For instance, Contemporary Amperex Technology Co. Limited (CATL), a well-known Chinese energy storage company, was founded in 2011. Just seven years later, it was listed on the ChiNext board of the Shenzhen Stock Exchange and quickly became the company with the largest market capitalization on the board, with its main business being energy storage batteries.

It is worth noting that the primary driving force behind the rapid development of battery energy storage technology has not come from the energy system but from the growth of electric vehicles. In the rapid advancement of electric vehicles, batteries are the most critical limiting factor. In the early stages of electric vehicle development, battery-based peak shaving for the grid seemed like a distant prospect. However, these two fields quickly converged, forming a powerful force in the energy revolution.

The rapid development of electric vehicles is a significant trend in the 21st century, bringing enormous changes to people's lives. In many cities, electric vehicles have become the top choice. Electric vehicles are not only potential massive electricity users but will inevitably become large-scale mobile energy storage stations in the future.

IEA recently released the report *Global EV Outlook 2019*. This annual report once again attests to the rapid growth in global EV sales (Figure 1-17). In 2018, global EV sales exceeded 2 million units, doubling from the previous year and pushing the cumulative global EV fleet past the 5 million mark to a record high of 5.1 million units—a year-on-year surge of 63%. Such a growth rate represents high-speed expansion even among emerging industries. The key drivers behind this trend remain policy support and technological advancements, particularly the continued improvement in battery performance and cost reductions, which continue to fuel sustained growth in the global EV market.

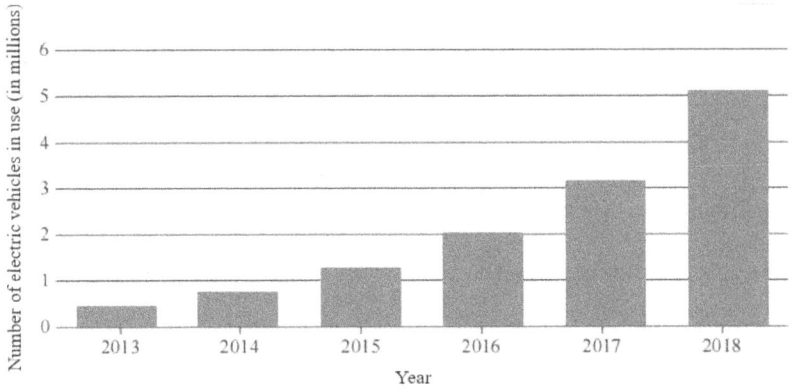

Figure 1-17 Global Stock of Electric Vehicles (Including Hybrid

Electric Vehicles) (Source: IEA)

On one hand, technological advancements are driving the rapid development of electric vehicles. On the other hand, air pollution and emissions are forcing governments to continuously strengthen clean energy policies, putting increasing pressure on traditional fuel vehicles. The year 2018 can be considered a watershed for the automotive industry, with many countries in Europe setting timelines for phasing out fuel vehicles. To date, countries such as the Netherlands, Norway, Paris (France), France, the United Kingdom, and India have all introduced specific bans on the sale of new fuel vehicles, with the earliest deadline being 2024 in Rome, Italy, and the latest being 2040 in the United Kingdom and France. Norway, the most aggressive promoter of electric vehicles, plans to completely ban non-electric vehicles by 2025. Given that nearly half of all new vehicles sold in Norway are already electric, this goal seems achievable. Even India has indicated that it is formulating a policy to promote the electric vehicle industry, aiming to stop selling pure gasoline and diesel vehicles nationwide and completely phase out internal combustion engine vehicles by 2030. Although the ban is still a decade away, its impact on consumer expectations and investment guidance is immediate. Major automakers have also begun to formulate plans to fully transition to new energy products. In July 2017, Volvo, a globally renowned automotive company, announced that it would produce only electric or hybrid vehicles by 2019, discontinuing the production of pure fuel vehicles. Volkswagen expects to achieve electrification by 2030, Toyota plans to stop producing fuel vehicles before 2025, and Jaguar Land Rover will offer only pure electric or hybrid models by 2020.

In China, there has been intense debate about the future of the automotive industry, but no definitive conclusion has been reached. In September 2017, leaders from the Ministry of Industry and Information Technology stated that research on a timeline for halting the production and sale of traditional energy vehicles had been initiated. In May 2019, the China Petroleum Consumption Cap and Policy Research Project released a report titled *Research on the Timeline for Phasing Out Traditional Fuel Vehicles in China* in Beijing. The report, prepared by the Innovation Center for Energy and Transportation (iCET), provided suggestions on the feasibility of implementing a ban on traditional fuel vehicles in China. Although the policy is still under discussion, the reality appears grim already. After more than two decades of rapid growth, traditional fuel passenger vehicles in China experienced negative sales growth for the first time in 2018, sending a strong signal to the market.

China holds the largest market share in global new electric vehicle sales, reaching 1.1 million units, accounting for more than half of the global total. Europe and the United States follow, with sales of 380,000 and 360,000 units, respectively. Among the 5.1 million electric vehicles in use worldwide, China has the largest installed base, with 2.3 million units, accounting for nearly half of the global total, making it the world's largest electric vehicle market. Europe and the United States rank second and third, with 1.2 million and 1.1 million units, respectively. In terms of electric vehicle market share, Nordic countries are leading the way. Norway, the pioneer, accounts for 46% of new vehicle sales with electric vehicles, the highest market share globally and nearly three times that of Iceland, which ranks second with a 17% market share. Sweden and the Netherlands rank third and fourth, with market shares of 8% and nearly 7%, respectively. Due to its large base, China's electric vehicle sales account for only about 4.5% of total vehicle sales.

The rapid development of electric vehicles has been accompanied by the rapid expansion of charging infrastructure (charging stations), which will provide assurance for long-distance travel by electric vehicles. In 2018, the number of electric vehicle charging infrastructure facilities (including public and private) worldwide was approximately 5.2 million, of which about 540,000 were public charging facilities. Nearly one-third of these public charging facilities are fast-charging stations, while the remaining two-thirds are slow-charging stations. Like electric vehicles, China also has the largest number of public charging facilities globally, with fast-charging stations accounting for about 40% of the global total and slow-charging stations accounting for as much as 78%.

Behind these numbers lie the unremitting efforts of the industry and policy support, with China being the undeniable leader. In early July 2019, a lively atmosphere pervaded Boao, Hainan, as the World New Energy Vehicle Congress opened with great fanfare. President Xi sent a congratulatory letter, praising the accelerated development of the new energy vehicle industry for injecting strong new momentum into economic growth in various countries and helping to reduce greenhouse gas emissions, address climate change challenges, and improve the global ecological environment. He particularly emphasized that China would adhere to the path of green, low-carbon, and sustainable development and accelerate the innovation and development of new energy vehicles and related industries.

When Wan Gang, the Vice Chairman of the Chinese People's Political Consultative Conference, appeared at the congress, he received warm applause. His decade-long efforts to promote the new energy vehicle industry have been fruitful, and the industry is now thriving. A memorable scene comes to mind: during the 2016 Clean Energy Ministerial Meeting,

Wan Gang, then the Minister of Science and Technology, initiated the "30%@30" national initiative for new energy vehicles, aiming to achieve a 30% share of new energy vehicles in new vehicle sales by 2030. Eight countries immediately responded, and China's leadership in this international initiative was a classic and impressive moment. Two years later, the achievements have exceeded expectations, with China's annual electric vehicle sales surpassing one million units. After traditional passenger vehicles in China experienced negative growth for the first time in 2018, the strategic importance of new energy vehicles has become even more prominent.

Electric vehicles are not only transforming the automotive industry but are also profoundly changing the energy landscape, although their current impact may seem negligible. Globally, in 2018, electric vehicles consumed only 0.2% of electricity and replaced a mere few hundred thousand barrels of oil per day, a negligible amount compared to the nearly 100 million barrels consumed globally each day. However, economic trends emerge at the margins or in terms of incremental changes. Considering the exponential growth trend of electric vehicles, the assessment of the situation changes completely.

According to forecasts by IEA, by 2030, the global installed base of electric vehicles will reach approximately 100 million units. This means that electricity consumption will reach 5%, and during specific periods, it may account for more than 20% of the total installed capacity. If not managed properly, this significant load change could easily cause grid collapse. Conversely, electric vehicles can also serve as natural energy storage devices. If they can provide intelligent peak shaving for the grid, electric vehicles can offer an enormous amount of peak shaving capacity, potentially eliminating the need for most peak shaving power stations.

This is the concept of Vehicle-to-Grid (V2G) technology, which enables interaction between electric vehicle batteries and the grid to optimize the value of the power system. V2G describes the relationship between electric vehicles and the grid. When electric vehicles are not in use, the electricity stored in their batteries can be sold to the grid. Conversely, when the batteries need charging, electricity flows from the grid to the vehicles. This process is based on the principle of maximizing value. Since electricity demand fluctuates constantly, the grid cannot store electricity and relies on real-time dispatch of generators to meet demand changes. With the increasing integration of unstable renewable energy sources into the grid, the challenge becomes even greater, making instantly available backup generation capacity increasingly valuable.

To put it more concretely, during the morning rush hour when electricity demand peaks, the grid needs to dispatch more generators and increase power generation. At night when factories are shut down and everyone is asleep, electricity demand drops, and the grid reduces the number of generators in operation and lowers power generation. This process can be simply understood as load regulation. If this regulation cannot keep up, it can lead to fluctuations in power frequency, such as from 50 Hz to 50.1 Hz or 49.9 Hz. In more severe cases, it can result in power outages, ranging from small-scale to large-scale blackouts. The batteries in electric vehicles serve as high-quality instant backup power sources. If properly managed, they can provide readily available backup capacity, much easier to start and stop than power plants. Since most vehicles are parked 95% of the time, their batteries can function as distributed energy storage units.

In August 2016, the world's first commercial V2G project was launched in Copenhagen. Although the scale was small, it was a typical cross-industry international cooperation project. The electric vehicle manufacturer was Nissan from Japan, the charging and discharging infrastructure was provided by Encl, a pioneer in new energy and smart grids in Europe, and Nuvve from California, a company dedicated to the research and development of V2G technology and services. Its platform, GIVe™, is specifically designed for vehicle-grid integration.

Frederiksberg Forsyning, a public service company in Copenhagen, served as the project owner. It installed 10 sets of Enel's V2G charging and discharging devices and purchased 10 Nissan zero-emission electric buses, the Nissan e-NV200. When the vehicles are not in use, they are plugged into the charging and discharging devices, allowing them to connect to the grid for charging and discharging at any time, becoming mobile energy stations for the grid. The available capacity of each vehicle's battery is approximately 10 kilowatts, providing a total capacity of around 100 kilowatts. Nuvve's platform is responsible for controlling the charging and discharging process. Developed initially by the University of Delaware, the platform ensures that the vehicles have sufficient power for normal operation while continuously optimizing the provision of reserve services, including frequency regulation, for the grid.

V2G also has a positive impact on existing business models. Frederiksberg Forsyning has actively participated in Denmark's energy management system through this project. Energinet.dk, Denmark's national grid operator, also hopes to promote this technology nationwide through the success of this demonstration project, thereby providing more stable grid services. In 2018, renewable energy accounted for 27.7% of Denmark's energy mix, with renewable energy generation accounting for nearly half, much higher than the global average. With a high proportion of renewable energy in the future, Denmark is also exploring experiences for the rest of the world.

Vehicle-grid integration projects are flourishing worldwide. In 2018, EV Consult released a dedicated industry report, stating that after years of research and demonstration, the era of commercial operation for V2G has arrived, based on a study of more than 50 V2G projects globally.

In early 2019, Renault announced the launch of a V2G charging pilot project, which utilizes alternating current (AC) charging stations, or slow-charging stations, to release electricity from vehicles to the grid for use by households, businesses, and public facilities. In 2019, Honda of Japan officially released its Wireless Vehicle-to-Grid technology, a bidirectional energy management system based on V2G vehicle networking. This technology wirelessly connects electric vehicles and plug-in hybrid vehicles to the power system, allowing them to charge and discharge simply by parking on a pad. This not only significantly improves the convenience of charging and discharging but also provides imagination space for future autonomous vehicles.

Not only electric vehicles but also fuel cells and hydrogen energy are attracting increasing attention. Traditionally, hydrogen has been used primarily as a chemical raw material, with global usage reaching approximately 800 billion cubic meters in 2018, a substantial amount. Hydrogen can also serve as an easily storable and transportable energy source, and exploration in this area has never ceased. During the oil crises of the 20th century, countries worldwide initiated peaks in hydrogen energy research. As the pressure of climate change increases in the 21st century, hydrogen energy development has once again gained attention.

There are various methods for hydrogen production. Traditionally, hydrogen has been produced through the pyrolysis of fossil fuels such as coal and natural gas. This hydrogen is known as "gray hydrogen" because its production increases carbon dioxide emissions. Hydrogen produced using carbon capture and storage (CCS) technology is called "blue hydrogen." With the rapid development of renewable energy, "green hydrogen" with zero emissions can be obtained through the electrolysis of water using renewable energy. Hydrogen also possesses enormous peak shaving capacity and can be used as a peak shaving energy storage method for renewable energy. Compared to batteries, hydrogen has a larger energy storage capacity and can be stored across seasons, serving as an important bridge to connect different energy sectors.

Hydrogen is also a high-calorific fuel. In Europe, there are already practices of injecting hydrogen produced from renewable energy directly into natural gas pipelines. In April 2019, Snam, Italy's national pipeline company, launched a demonstration project to blend 5% hydrogen into natural gas. Located in Salerno Province, Italy, the project supplies hydrogen-blended gas to two local enterprises, including the renowned pasta manufacturer Orogillo. Orogillo proudly announced on its official promotional page that it produces the world's first pasta fueled by hydrogen. If all the gas supplied by Snam were blended with 5% hydrogen, it would require 3.5 billion cubic meters of hydrogen annually and reduce carbon dioxide emissions by 2.5 million tons. The significance of this experiment lies in its ability to test the compatibility of existing infrastructure with hydrogen. If hydrogen can be well integrated and substituted for natural gas, the application scenarios for hydrogen will expand significantly, and it will be compatible with existing infrastructure. According to practices in Norway, blending up to 10% hydrogen is also feasible. If the material of gas pipelines is upgraded, the Norwegian classification society is also researching scenarios with a 30% hydrogen blend. Theoretically, if the gas pipeline material is plastic, hydrogen can be blended up to 100%. Of course, these application scenarios also require careful consideration of user-side demand. Natural gas is also an important peak shaving energy source. In the energy transition, natural gas can continue to play a significant role not only because it is relatively clean but also because it is an important potential source of flexibility.

Hydrogen can be well integrated with electricity through fuel cells for power generation, serving not only as a flexible energy storage but also as an excellent peak shaving power source. This is why many countries and institutions have high hopes for hydrogen, as it can smoothly convert with all existing energy systems, bringing greater flexibility to the system. In a system with a high proportion of renewable energy, increasing system flexibility is undoubtedly highly valuable. However, a large number of backup hydrogen fuel cells also means increased costs. If combined with the daily applications of fuel cell vehicles, the prospects for industrialization appear promising, similar to the case of chemical batteries.

The development of fuel cells will objectively compete with chemical batteries and pure electric vehicles, with scale cost-effectiveness being a key factor. Therefore, seizing strategic high ground is crucial. Japan is at the forefront in this regard. At the 2019 G20 Energy Ministers' Meeting in Japan, hydrogen energy was the most discussed energy topic. To this end, the Japanese government supported IEA in publishing a report titled *The Future of Hydrogen,* which systematically reviewed the development status and opportunities of hydrogen energy. The report was officially released during the meeting and received attention from governments and institutions worldwide.

The Japanese government's strong support for hydrogen energy reflects its distinctive national energy strategy. As Japan lacks domestically produced energy and relies almost entirely on imports for its oil and natural gas, energy security concerns have permeated its national strategy. Even after the Fukushima incident, Japan did not abandon nuclear power decisively because it considers nuclear power a reliable local energy source. From this perspective, it is easy to understand Japan's perseverance in developing hydrogen energy for decades, as it can be seen as a local energy resource. Hydrogen energy is not only crucial for Japan's clean energy development but also serves as a pillar of its energy security. Japan is also exploring the import of hydrogen produced in countries such as Australia and Brunei to further diversify its energy supply.

Competition between technology routes often goes beyond the technologies themselves, with business models and policies playing a crucial role. Hydrogen fuel cells and chemical batteries serve as a typical example, as their industrial chains are long. Once infrastructure and markets gain an advantage, the industry will experience a "Matthew effect," where the dominant party leverages economies of scale to further widen its advantage, creating stronger exclusivity. This is why, during the process of technological competition, related industries often strive to elevate their status to a national strategy. If the assessment is accurate, national support can significantly accelerate this process, enabling domestic companies to gain an international advantage. Of course, there are also many cases where the assessment is inaccurate, carrying some elements of venture capital. In the development of renewable energy such as wind and photovoltaic power, China's proactive support policies serve as a successful example. In the development of hydrogen energy, many relevant countries have also formulated highly proactive support policies, and some local governments have enthusiastically embraced them, with enterprises springing up like mushrooms. However, whether these efforts can achieve results similar to those in the new energy sector remains to be tested by the market.

The development of new energy is no longer dominated solely by renewable energy. Driven by digitalization, new energy business models are emerging, integrating electricity, gas, energy storage, and other sectors to an unprecedented extent. This integration significantly improves energy efficiency, reduces emissions, and provides a powerful tool for humanity to

address climate change.

Part II

Digital Transformation of Energy

Digital technology has profoundly changed our lives, but its impact on energy is just beginning to unfold, with its power accumulating and poised to drive energy from mere supply to comprehensive service, a substantive manifestation of the energy revolution.

People often become overly absorbed in the present moment and need to frequently reflect on history in order to face the future. On September 3, 1999, some media outlets and early internet companies initiated an event called the "72-Hour Internet Survival Test," aimed at promoting the application of the internet. Twelve volunteers participating in this event were placed in separate rooms in Beijing, Guangzhou, and Shanghai, relying solely on the internet to meet their survival needs. These volunteers endured hunger and cold; some subsisted on soy milk for three days, while others dropped out after going hungry for two days. This event became a landmark scene marking the beginning of the internet's development in China. At that time, internet speed, online services, and supporting services such as delivery were incomparable to today's standards, and ordering food online was far less reliable than making a phone call.

In just one or two decades, the remarkable changes have been evident to all. Seventeen years later, during the Mobile World Congress held in Shanghai, the organizers paid tribute to the 1999 event by hosting a creative "72-Hour Offline Living Test." The volunteers who participated in this activity ultimately reported that they were nearly "driven to the brink" after three days without internet access.

Internet technology is revolutionizing every traditional industry, altering many fundamental operational frameworks, and transforming people's lives. The core concept of the internet is sharing, which has significantly reduced transaction costs and spurred the emergence and transformation of numerous new industries. For instance, the world's largest "hotel" has no physical rooms (Airbnb), and the largest "car rental" company owns no vehicles (Uber). This has prompted the vast majority of traditional industries to undergo upgrades and transformations. However, for the energy industry, such changes are only just beginning to unfold (Figure 2-1).

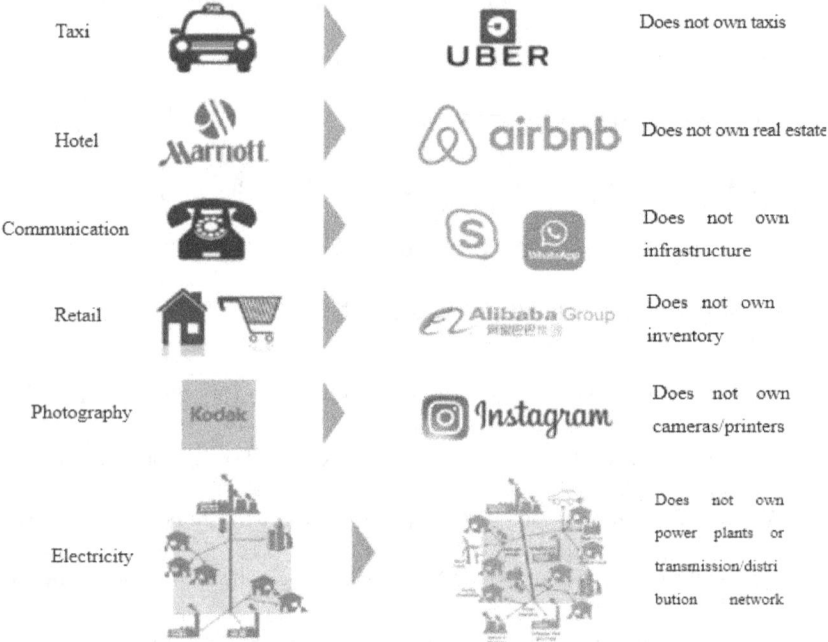

Figure 2-1 Stephen, Chief Digital Officer at Poyry Consulting in the UK, has created a starkly contrasting diagram that highlights the profound transformations brought about by digitization and the internet across numerous industries. Notably, the energy sector is only at the nascent stage of such changes (Source: Poyry).

The Wave of Energy Digitization

The book *The Third Industrial Revolution* keenly recognizes that internet technology will significantly transform the energy structure, with renewable energy making rapid progress in tandem with the development of internet technology. Nine years have passed, and the actual progress has been even faster than anticipated. New energy technologies are advancing rapidly, with costs plummeting. Meanwhile, the cost-effectiveness of related digital technologies such as sensors, storage devices, and broadband has improved even more rapidly than that of new energy. Concepts like energy internet, smart energy, and energy Internet of Things (IoT) are flourishing and gaining increasing attention, heralding a promising era of significant development. It can be said that the development of information technology has laid a solid foundation for large-scale digitalization in the energy industry.

What deserves particular attention is the digitalization and intelligence on the consumption side. Digitalization empowers energy consumers with unprecedented capabilities, enabling them not only to utilize energy more intelligently and efficiently but also to more conveniently leverage various distributed energy technologies to become prosumer consumers—both producers and consumers of energy. Digitalization has propelled them to the forefront of driving the energy revolution. The intelligence on the consumption side starts from the end and forces the restructuring of the entire energy system. Within the framework of a market economy, energy consumers are finally gradually returning to their rightful dominant position.

The digitalization of energy has attracted the attention of governments and enterprises worldwide, although the degree of attention may vary significantly. The theme report of the 2017 International Energy Agency Energy Ministers' Meeting was "Energy and Digitalization." Interestingly this report first took stock of the top ten companies by market capitalization globally. In stark contrast to a decade ago, when energy companies dominated the list, technology companies centered around data and intelligence have now comprehensively replaced energy companies. Two years later, this trend has become even more pronounced, with ExxonMobil, the only remaining energy industry leader on the list, also being ousted (Figure 2-2).

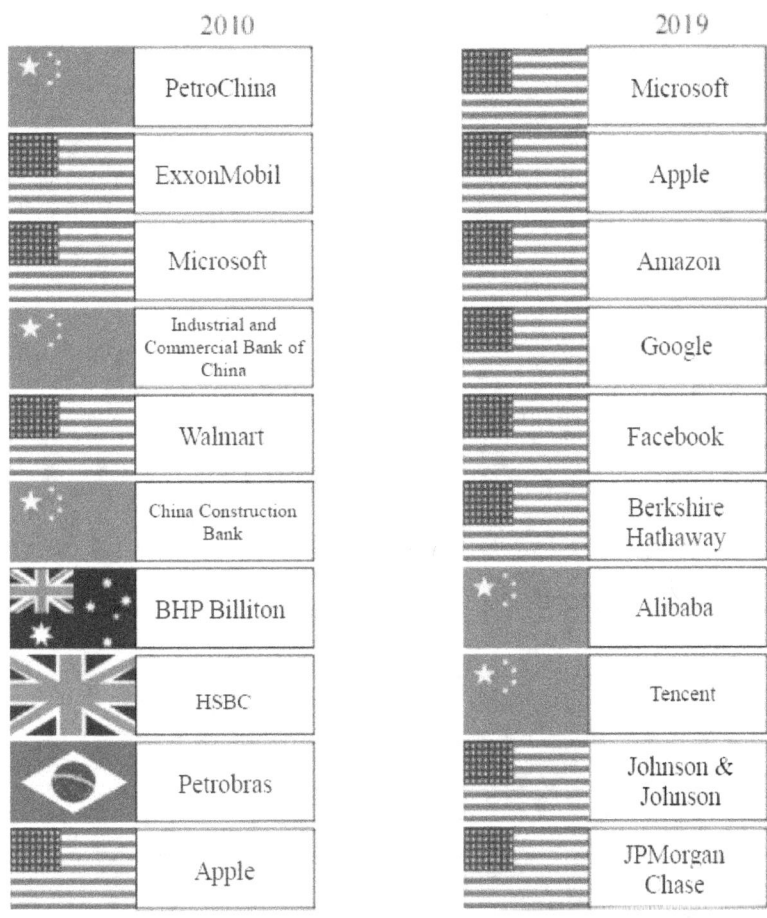

Figure 2-2 Comparative Chart of Changes in the World's Highest Market Capitalization Companies (Compiled Based on Online Data)

In 2010, three of the top ten companies globally by market capitalization were energy companies. By 2019, no energy companies were on the list, with information technology companies occupying all the top five positions.

This shift in the rankings also conveys an important message: technology is becoming increasingly valuable. While possessing oil and natural gas resources used to be the foundation for maintaining energy security, technology is now increasingly becoming the cornerstone of energy security.

Masayoshi Son, the founder of SoftBank, a flagship internet investment company, in his latest speech, cited two images to illustrate the rapid changes in life during periods of breakthrough technological progress or technological revolutions, images that are also favored by Amory B. Lovins, the founder of the Rocky Mountain Institute (Figures 2-3 and 2-4).

Figure 2-3 Street Scene of New York City on Easter Morning, 1900

Note: This photograph, sourced from the U.S. National Archives, was taken on Easter morning along New York's famed Fifth Avenue in 1900.

The bustling streets were filled with horse-drawn carriages during the holiday, but within the circled area lies a novelty—an automobile. In 1900, automobiles were still a recent invention, often ridiculed for their impracticality, such as the lack of refueling stations. This echoes modern criticisms of electric vehicles, suggesting deeper resistance rooted in unfamiliarity with transformative technologies that are poised to reshape lifestyles, much like the transition from horse-drawn carriages did.

Figure 2-4 Street Scene of New York City on Easter Morning, 1913

Note: Thirteen years later, at nearly the same location and during the same holiday, the bustling streets remain crowded—but now dominated entirely by automobiles. Interestingly, a lone horse-drawn carriage lingers in a similar corner as before. The Second Industrial Revolution, symbolized by the automobile, transformed transportation in just over a decade. History repeats itself with striking parallelism.

Masayoshi Son lamented that such periods of technological revolution are once-in-a-century opportunities for the investment field. He has been fortunate enough to experience two such periods: the internet at the end of the 20th century and the ongoing AI (artificial intelligence) revolution. Looking back, the internet has dramatically transformed our lives in just over a decade. He predicts that AI will also profoundly change people's lives. To vividly illustrate this point, he added a scene of Fifth Avenue in 2035 to his speech, where self-driving cars will dominate the streets (Figure 2-5).

Figure 2-5 Schematic Diagram of Future Transportation

Note: This represents Masayoshi Son's vision for the future of transportation. From an investor's perspective, it presents tremendous investment opportunities. From the viewpoint of an energy expert, it also entails a vast number of mobile energy storage stations. Autonomous electric vehicles will not only serve as means of transportation but also function as mobile energy nodes, constituting a crucial component of the energy IoT.

It can be said that the intelligentization of transportation and the digitalization of energy share similar paths. The development of energy digitalization also inevitably requires the large-scale application of artificial intelligence. One of the greatest advantages of AI is analysis and prediction. The large-scale development of new-generation distributed energy, renewable energy, energy storage, and smart users all rely on big data analysis and prediction. Intelligence is one of the core supports for the large-scale development of these new energy technologies (Figures 2-6 and 2-7).

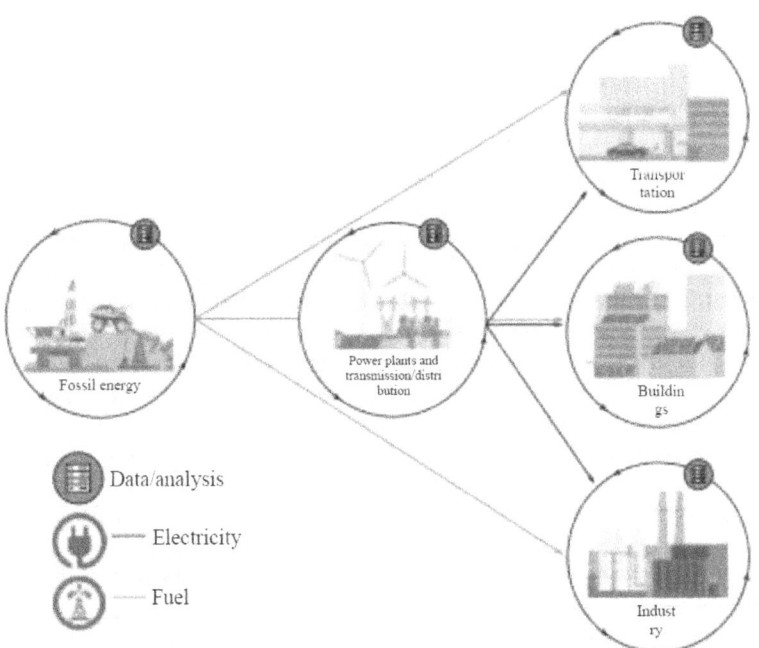

Figure 2-6 This is a structural diagram of traditional energy and power supply. Digitalization can enhance efficiency in each link, but these links remain relatively independent (Source: IEA).

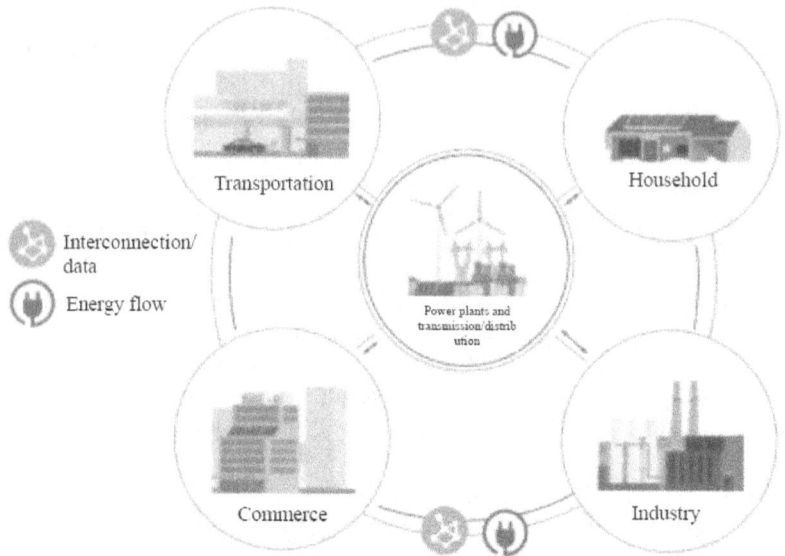

Figure 2-7 This is a structural diagram of energy and power supply-demand with data interconnection. Digitalization has reshaped the entire energy supply-demand landscape, breaking down the boundaries between supply and demand, thereby enabling support for a greater number of energy prosumers. Similar to information flow, the flow of energy has become bidirectional rather than unidirectional (Source: IEA).

The energy industry was among the earliest to benefit from digitalization. Decades ago, power plants and oil and gas fields began applying information technologies such as computers to improve automation and management levels. Now, concepts like digital power plants and digital oil fields have been proposed, significantly enhancing labor productivity and reducing manual labor.

Currently, all major international oil companies are promoting further digitalization. For example, by utilizing remote video monitoring and various sensors for temperature and pressure, an increasing number of unmanned oil field well sites are emerging. The widespread use of these data technologies has made many remote operations easier. For instance, in Shell's Vaca Muerta oil field development project in Argentina, the company relied on digital means to conduct remote drilling. Engineers in Calgary, Canada, remotely controlled the drilling speed and pressure through real-time data feedback, improving technical levels while significantly reducing exploration costs. The coal industry is also using smart mine software to more intuitively manage and optimize the development process, thereby increasing production capacity.

However, strictly speaking, these digitalization efforts on the production side are only the beginning on a local scale. With the rapid development and cost reduction of information technology, it is reconstructing the energy system from broader and deeper perspectives, systematically transforming the entire energy industry chain and ecosystem from production to consumption. This integration will organically connect every link in the chain, greatly improving energy utilization efficiency, which is the essence of the energy revolution.

For the power industry, digitalization brings more extensive changes, from power plants and transmission and distribution to the user end, with closer connections at each link in the industry chain. It is reported that the Netherlands has promoted large-scale digital transformation of its power network, using information-integrated big data and prediction technologies to provide better services. A total of 1.5 billion various sensors have been used in the transmission and distribution network. Given the scale of the Netherlands' power system, one can imagine the magnitude of this digitalization project.

From the perspective of power users, the widely promoted smart meters are more tangible. With smart meters installed, users can directly pay their bills online or via mobile phones. The value of smart meters goes beyond this; through them, power grid companies can collect power consumption data in real-time, better schedule power supply through big data analysis, and respond more sensitively to demand changes.

Traditional energy companies have accumulated vast amounts of data through digitalization on the production side, relying on big data and cloud platforms. This digitalization on the production side has laid the groundwork for systemic changes across the entire industry chain, especially for accommodating more unstable renewable energy and more flexible consumption-side responses.

In March 2017, China Southern Power Grid completed the construction of the first "Internet + Smart Energy Comprehensive Demonstration Community" project based on the integration of four networks (power grid, internet, TV network, and telephone network) in the Guangzhou Zhongxin Knowledge City within its service area. The project covers 21 buildings with approximately 1,450 households. The physical foundation of the entire project is the integration of power optical fibers into households. Fiber-optic composite low-voltage cables combine optical cables with power cables, integrating the power grid, internet, TV network, and telephone network into a single network through access to different operators' networks. This integration enables the transmission and interconnection of different types of energy flows and information flows, such as power and energy data and smart home control data. The technological key to the project is the intelligent transformation of electricity, water, and gas meters. The data from these three meters are remotely transmitted and copied through unified collection devices and dedicated optical fiber networks within the community, completing the meter reading for all users in a building in just 10 seconds, significantly improving accuracy and efficiency. Simultaneously, it enables real-time remote control and fault diagnosis, analysis of system losses, and integrated and intelligent management of electricity, water, and gas meters, including "reading, calculation, management, and control." The system records electricity consumption down to the level of individual appliances at different times. For example, it can provide detailed electricity consumption data for lights, refrigerators, TVs, air conditioners, and other appliances at different times of the day, laying the foundation for an in-depth understanding of user needs through big data analysis. Furthermore, based on the integration of the four networks and the centralized reading of the three meters, combined with other modules such as distributed energy, charging facilities, smart homes, and smart community comprehensive management systems, it deeply integrates energy and information, generating vast amounts of data on electricity, water, and gas consumption. This data provides insights into users' energy consumption habits, structures, and characteristics, enabling the reasonable optimization of users' electricity, water, and gas consumption expenditures. Taking this as a starting point, combined with smart home technologies with different scene modes, this project can be upgraded and promoted to other communities and applied to the production sector. For example, in enterprise production processes, it can analyze the energy consumption levels, structures, and time periods of each electrical equipment, as well as optimize the energy consumption structures for different warehousing facilities' temperature and humidity requirements.

Traditional energy consumers have often been passive recipients, lacking choices and a voice for a long time. However, new-generation technologies such as smart homes, distributed energy, and electric vehicles provide energy consumers with more options. The popularity of smart homes not only brings more convenience to life but also significantly enhances the ability of the consumption side to respond and interact with the power grid.

According to rough statistics, there are currently nearly 20 billion smart home devices that can be connected to the internet globally. Smart homes provide information interaction functions through the internet, creating conditions for the rational use of energy. For example, they can automatically perform tasks like laundry and charging during off-peak hours. Through smart microgrids, energy suppliers can also interact with these flexible energy-using units, achieving energy supply-demand balance at the lowest possible cost.

The most crucial support for digitalization on the energy consumption side is the continuous maturation of smart microgrids. Since the concept of microgrids was proposed by the Consortium for Electric Reliability Technology Solutions (CERTS) in the United States decades ago, microgrids have made significant progress, although specific definitions may vary in emphasis, their basic connotations are consistent: a smart microgrid is a small-scale power generation and distribution system that integrates distributed power sources, energy storage devices, energy conversion devices, related loads, and monitoring and protection devices. It is an autonomous system capable of self-control, protection, and management, which can operate both in parallel with the external power grid and in isolation.

Smart microgrids are a modernized and miniaturized form of large-scale power systems, capable of more personalizedly meeting users' growing demands, maximizing the utilization of clean energy, and promoting technological innovation. Smart microgrids can intelligently optimize and manage various energy generation equipment and end-user equipment. By adopting advanced power technologies, communication technologies, computer technologies, and control technologies, they meet the higher development needs of future power, energy, environment, and economy in distribution networks while fulfilling existing distribution network functions. The application of smart microgrids will also provide better conditions for energy integration and modern energy services. Energy services such as heating, power supply, cooling, gas supply, and hot water supply all occur on the consumption side. Therefore, only with more flexible collaboration on the consumption side can energy be supplied in the most efficient and clean manner.

The metropolis of New York has set an ambitious energy development vision for itself: by 2030, 70% of New York's electricity supply will come from renewable sources. This requires higher energy efficiency and reliable renewable energy access, not just increasing the renewable energy ratio but upgrading the entire system. To this end, New York Governor Andrew M. Cuomo has led the formulation of a comprehensive energy reform strategy, Reforming the Energy Vision (REV), aimed at enabling consumers to better understand their energy options and promoting the development of new energy products and services. This will also involve significant adjustments to the energy policy framework.

Energy digitalization is not only rapidly advancing at the company and city levels but can also be elevated to a national strategy. In the digital revolution in the energy field, there is a small country that stands out—Estonia. This small Nordic country may be unfamiliar to many, but it has taken the lead in proposing a digital nation strategy and is at the forefront of energy digitalization worldwide.

WePower, a Latvian company established just two years ago, has been listed among the top ten most innovative global energy companies. In 2018, WePower collaborated with Elering, an Estonian power transmission company, to launch a pilot project to upgrade the national energy system using blockchain technology.

An important task of this project was to transfer energy production and consumption data equivalent to one year in Estonia to a blockchain database. During the pilot phase, a cumulative 26,000 hours and 24 TWh of energy production and consumption data were converted into 39 billion blockchain data points.

Estonia's nationwide energy data tokenization pilot enabled WePower to test the application capabilities of blockchain technology, thereby establishing a reliable platform, achieving the transaction of the first green energy procurement project, and developing a market platform for medium- and large-scale energy transactions.

Why has Estonia been able to advance so far in this field? In its digitalization strategy promoted over the years, the country has already established a vast energy data infrastructure, and the digital transformation of the power grid has been completed. Elering's Estfeed energy database has prepared sufficient data, including a large amount of electricity and gas data. When upgrading this data with blockchain technology, much of the groundwork had already been completed. Similar energy digitalization projects are increasingly being carried out in more and more countries.

From the perspective of promoting renewable energy development, the high-proportion integration of renewable energy also urgently requires digital support. The scale of individual renewable energy power sources is often small, especially for distributed renewable energy, which is even smaller. Managing them through conventional methods would require a large workforce and would not meet efficiency requirements, making digitalization an inevitable choice. Nowadays, there are more and more unmanned wind farms and photovoltaic power stations, all of which rely on digital support.

In supporting distributed energy transactions, the widespread application of blockchain technology provides strong support for small-scale energy transactions. The application of blockchain technology in the energy industry, especially in direct transactions between users, will be further discussed later. It enables transactions to be conducted directly without intermediaries, significantly reducing transaction costs. Blockchain technology will bring about tremendous changes not only in the energy sector but also in many other industries such as finance.

The application of drones in the energy industry is also a scenario for digitalization. A-Style, a Japanese company originally focused on roofing and exterior construction, successfully transformed its business more than a decade ago with the popularization of residential photovoltaic systems in Japan. In addition to providing photovoltaic Engineering, Procurement, and Construction (EPC) services, operation and maintenance, and independent power sales businesses, it also offers operational monitoring system services, including using drones to detect faults in solar panels. Drones can use infrared cameras and image analysis technologies to detect the condition of photovoltaic panels. Monitoring personnel can identify issues with the power station by comparing the images and hotspots captured by the infrared camera with those of surrounding panels. Generally, relatively high-temperature positions may indicate some kind of fault. Of course, the reasons for increased panel temperatures vary, including panel and connection faults, as well as dirt and bird droppings. In recent years, the costs of drones and related monitoring facilities have rapidly decreased. In addition to hardware, various AI learning and data analysis software systems are constantly being updated, creating conditions for the large-scale application of drones in the energy industry.

Envision Energy, a large wind turbine manufacturer in China, is also a pioneer in energy digitalization. It first significantly improved the digitalization level of wind turbines and then launched the EnOS™ energy IoT platform in September 2016. Utilizing advanced technologies such as IoT, cloud computing, and big data, the platform connects and manages various power generation, consumption, energy storage, and transmission and distribution equipment. Its goal is to enable coordinated operation of energy equipment in every household, community, and even every city, reduce investment costs on the power generation side, achieve precise monitoring and management of loads, and realize energy supply-demand balance according to market dynamics (Figure 2-8).

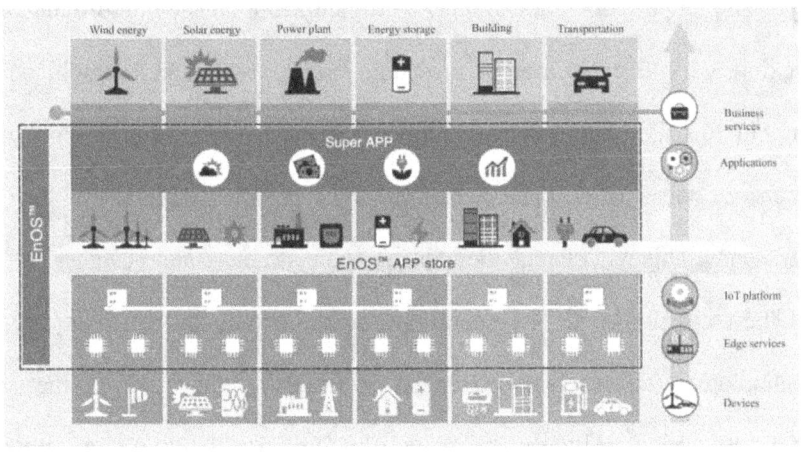

Figure 2-8 Schematic Diagram of Envision EnOS™ Platform (Source: Envision Energy)

Note: The Envision EnOS™ platform can connect and manage a range of power generation equipment and end-users, enabling collaborative operation at the household, community, and city levels.

To meet peak load demands, the power system needs to prepare a considerable amount of redundant power generation capacity to ensure that peak demands can be met, even if these peaks only last for an hour or even just a few minutes. This actually results in significant waste, with a substantial portion of power generation capacity idle most of the time. If the demand-side response capability can be better utilized, with the help of digital technology, peak shaving and valley filling can be achieved, thereby reducing investment in reserve power generation capacity (Figure 2-9).

The important value of energy digitalization lies in improving the flexibility of the entire system, providing energy services more intelligently and in real-time according to energy demands, and instantly supplying energy services at the lowest cost, thereby significantly improving energy efficiency. This will change the industry chain structure and business model of the entire industry. The energy sector has witnessed many large-scale technological advancements over the past century, but this time, the task may not necessarily be completed by traditional energy companies themselves.

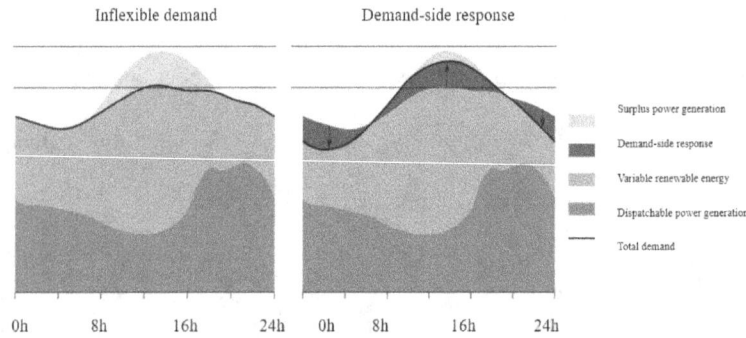

Figure 2-9 Schematic Diagram of Enhancing System Flexibility through Demand-Side Response (Source: IEA)

Energy Ventures of Information Companies

Traditionally, energy companies worldwide have focused their attention on their assets (production facilities and transmission and distribution networks) rather than on customers. Energy companies have been more akin to production units than marketing units. The concept of "outsourced production," which is prevalent in most manufacturing industries, is largely foreign to the energy sector. Marketing by energy suppliers to customers often centers on price, rather than adopting the consumer-centric, differentiated, and personalized approaches common in most other mass-market industries. Even in the relatively digitally advanced electricity sector, internal organizational structures and customer relationships remain highly traditional, seemingly out of touch with the Internet age. However, the rapid digitalization of the energy industry has created opportunities for companies proficient in data operations. These companies can establish direct relationships with end consumers, enabling them to offer new services and generate revenue. Of course, they can also purchase energy products from traditional energy providers through outsourcing.

Compared to the digital upgrades of traditional energy companies, IT companies have adopted vastly different strategies when entering the digital energy sector. Lacking existing energy assets, they start with a clean slate and typically begin directly in the renewable energy sector. Beyond ideological factors such as addressing climate change and promoting green development, there is also a natural technological fit, as digitalization inherently offers advantages in managing the variability of renewable energy sources like wind and solar power.

DeepMind, a subsidiary of Google headquartered in London, announced in early 2019 that it could predict the power output of wind farms up to 36 hours in advance using artificial intelligence. This allows for better alignment with market demand, thereby enhancing the value of wind farms. Although this technology does not increase the amount of wind power generated, the improved predictability significantly reduces the negative impact of uncertainty on the system and decreases the likelihood of wind power curtailment. According to DeepMind's assessment, this AI-based prediction technology increased the value of wind farms by 20% (Figure 2-10).

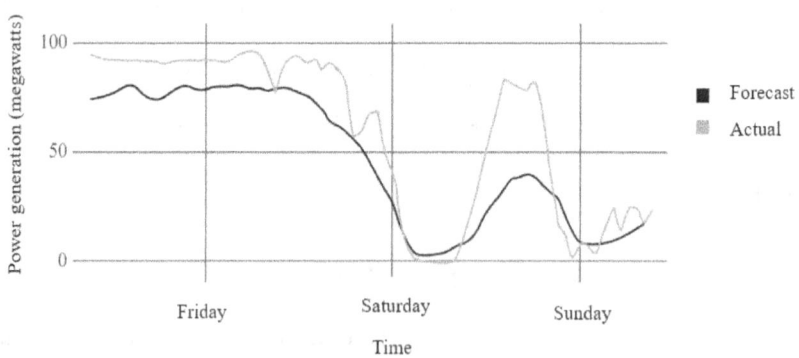

Figure 2-10 Schematic Diagram of Wind Farm Power Generation

Forecast by Shensi Company (Source: DeepMind)

Note: This is a display by DeepMind showing the 72-hour power generation forecast versus actual output for a wind farm. As can be seen, wind power exhibits significant fluctuations. To be honest, judging by the forecasting performance in this graph, there are still some discrepancies between the forecasted curve and the actual output, especially as the forecast horizon extends further into the future. Nevertheless, it has still significantly improved the wind farm's efficiency, demonstrating the immense potential that lies in the integration of digitalization with new energy sources.

This is not Google's first foray into using AI for energy management. In 2016, Google reduced its energy consumption by 15% through AI. Google was also among the first multinational corporations to commit to using 100% renewable energy, achieving this goal in 2018 through a combination of building its own distributed renewable energy systems and purchasing green energy.

Google's strategic direction increasingly involves tracking renewable energy usage, improving its efficiency, and finding new positions within the rapidly evolving energy system. Although DeepMind has not yet generated profits for Google and incurred losses exceeding $300 million in 2017, Google's support has not hindered DeepMind's continued research and development efforts.

Google's involvement in new energy continues to expand. Skycatch, an emerging U.S. company founded in 2013 that specializes in drone applications, received investment from Google during its seed funding stage. Leading photovoltaic companies SolarCity and First Solar subsequently contracted Skycatch to use drones for inspection and monitoring of PV power plants.

Skycatch's quadcopter drones are equipped with autonomous navigation GPS, sonar technology, and infrared cameras, enabling precise location and inspection of faults. When the battery runs low or storage is full, the drone automatically returns to its base landing box. Upon landing, a robotic arm replaces the used battery with a new one and uploads the data, allowing Skycatch's clients to access the latest data almost in real time.

While the intelligent management of wind farms and PV power plants can be seen as extensions of traditional power generation businesses, Google's 2014 acquisition of NEST Labs represents a deeper strategic move.

Founded in 2010 by former Apple engineers Tony Fadell and Matt Rogers, NEST Labs is dedicated to creating smart home devices. Its flagship product, launched the following year, was a programmable, self-learning indoor thermostat that could be controlled by detectors and connected to WiFi. Even when occupants are away, they can control the thermostat via a mobile app, enabling remote temperature adjustments to turn off air conditioning or heating when leaving and turn it back on before returning home. Following this internet-centric approach, NEST subsequently introduced a series of products, including smoke detectors and carbon monoxide detectors. The company grew rapidly, employing 120 people by the end of 2012, and was acquired by Google for $3.2 billion in early 2014. This acquisition exemplifies the growth of a typical "American Dream" unicorn company, achieving billionaire status in just four years.

With NEST, Google can further grasp changes in energy demand. Through big data analysis, it becomes easy to understand customers' energy usage patterns, such as when they return home and their preferred room temperatures. Data from thousands of households can more clearly outline energy consumption curves (Figure 2-11).

Figure 2-11 Promotional Image of Google's NEST

Note: This small thermostat is a prime example of applying Internet thinking in the energy sector, featuring self-learning capabilities (Image Source: Google).

When this data is linked to variable wind and solar power, its value becomes evident. For example, as the sun sets and PV power generation ceases, while occupants return home and turn on heating, identifying the most convenient and cost-effective energy sources for this period presents a significant business opportunity. This energy could come from instantly start-up natural gas power plants, ground-source heat pumps, or additional power generated by strong winds, as accurately forecasted by weather predictions. It could also be sourced from electric vehicles parked in garages and connected to the grid. Big data calculations can easily identify the most economical energy source, creating substantial value. If the energy market functions efficiently, this value will be reflected in price differentials, allowing companies to reap substantial profits.

Not only IT companies like Google but also innovative firms like Tesla are making significant strides into the energy sector.

Elon Musk's brilliance lies in striving to be a pioneer rather than a martyr, leading to unprecedented success across multiple crossover fields. Energy appears to be no exception, with Musk's energy focus clearly and explicitly centered on energy storage and PV power.

Just as high-end smartphones aim to be artistic masterpieces rather than mere phones, with Apple being a prime example, Tesla Energy has given PV panels a new look. Although many PV companies have attempted similar designs, Tesla stands out as highly representative.

Tesla offers four types of PV tiles: Textured, Smooth, Tuscan, and Slate. At first glance, these tiles are indistinguishable from those found in decoration markets. This fusion of renewable green energy with fashionable living represents a new direction for PV panels. Given the rapid price reductions driven by technological advancements, the early adoption of such fashionable designs is unlikely to pose significant price barriers for high-end users.

Tesla's PV tiles are made of tempered glass, boasting more than triple the strength of standard tiles. The company's website features engaging comparative videos demonstrating their durability. While these videos may be seen as promotional gimmicks, Tesla's generous warranty terms are more substantial, offering a lifetime warranty for the tiles as long as the house stands and a 30-year warranty for their power generation capabilities.

Tesla's sleek Powerwall storage system also exudes a sense of style. It can store solar-generated electricity and, thanks to its built-in inverter, serve as a backup power source to meet household electricity demands. If necessary, it can even operate independently of the grid, functioning as a standalone battery for emergency power. Each Powerwall has a capacity of

13.5 kWh, and up to ten units can be combined, far exceeding the needs of most households.

An even more convenient energy storage solution offered by Tesla is the battery in its electric vehicles. When parked in a garage, a Tesla vehicle can be transformed into a small power station through bidirectional charging facilities (Figure 2-12).

Figure 2-12 Tesla's Energy Model Diagram

(Image Source: Tesla's Official Website)

Note: This widely circulated image depicts Tesla's conceptual model for future home energy, where photovoltaics, energy storage, and electric vehicles enable household energy self-sufficiency. This green energy independence is not just about energy; it also serves as a lifestyle statement to express one's individuality.

SolarCity, a subsidiary of Tesla producing PV components, was acquired by Musk in 2016. Founded in 2006 by Peter and Lyndon Rive, based on the guidance and support of their cousin Musk, this company focused on residential PV products rapidly expanded through acquisitions, becoming the second-largest PV installer in the United States by 2013. In 2016, Tesla acquired SolarCity for $2.6 billion, with Musk stating the move was "to seamlessly integrate PV power and energy storage." However, some critics accused Musk of assisting his cousins.

Tesla is difficult to classify solely as an automotive company. If a label must be applied, it could be considered an IT company, an energy company, and an automotive company, embodying the "Internet+" concept advocated by former Premier Li Keqiang. For Tesla, automobiles are merely carriers with automotive functions that integrate smart homes, energy supply, the IoT, and all related information. It is this integration of information that creates the conditions for providing energy efficiently in the most economical and clean manner (Figure 2-13).

Figure 2-13 Tesla's photovoltaic and energy storage have achieved a

significant scale (Image Source: Tesla's official website)

These IT companies' forays into the energy sector have initially demonstrated a style vastly different from that of traditional energy companies. The dust stirred up by these "gray rhinos" is clearly visible, and the era of the energy internet will arrive more swiftly with their participation.

The Energy Internet

American renowned economist Jeremy Rifkin first proposed the concept of the "Energy Internet" in his book *The Third Industrial Revolution*: "We need to create an Energy Internet that enables millions of people to produce green, renewable energy in their homes, offices, and factories. Surplus energy can be shared with others, just as we share information on the Internet today." Rifkin's concept of the "Energy Internet" has received significant attention from former Premier Li Keqiang and has been widely echoed within China's energy sector.

The Energy Internet is not a nebulous concept. With the rapid advancement of Internet and renewable energy technologies, smart microgrids and distributed energy systems have sprung up, laying a solid foundation for the Energy Internet. Governments and institutions in the United States, Europe, Japan, China, and other countries have conducted extensive research on aspects similar to the Energy Internet.

In 2008, Alex Q. Huang from North Carolina State University in the United States led The Future Renewable Electric Energy Delivery and Management Systems (FREEDM) project, a National Science Foundation initiative. The project aimed to further integrate power electronics and information technology into the power system, implementing Internet concepts at the future distribution network level. Emulating the core routers in computer network technology, they proposed the concept of the energy-router.

After research and refinement, the China Electric Power Research Institute defined the "energy-router" as an intelligent entity that integrates the cyber-physical systems of the power grid. It possesses capabilities such as computing, communication, precise control, remote coordination, autonomy, and universal plug-and-play access. Its basic characteristics include:

Adopting a fully flexible solid-state device architecture;

Combining the functions of traditional transformers, circuit breakers, power flow control devices, and power quality control devices;

Enabling seamless AC-DC hybrid power distribution and consumption;

Allowing plug-and-play access for distributed power sources and flexible loads (such as distributed energy storage and electric vehicles);

Featuring an intelligent control unit with information fusion for autonomous distributed control operation and energy management;

Integrating a robust communication network function.

The energy-router will have a series of functions including energy interaction, intelligent distribution, and buffered energy storage.

The energy-router can be regarded as a device with distinct Internet characteristics, and its name is derived from Internet terminology. The realization of the energy router relies not only on advancements in power electronics technology but also on the development of large-scale energy storage technologies. Energy storage serves as a cache in the Energy Internet. Although large-scale energy storage still requires further solutions to technical issues such as efficiency, cost, and capacity, a range of energy storage technologies, including battery storage, mechanical storage, and hydrogen (natural gas) storage, are flourishing. The combination of large-scale energy storage technologies and power electronics will continuously optimize the functions of the energy router. Given that the application scenarios of energy-routers are more complex and harder to standardize than those of Internet routers, it is currently difficult to claim that a standard energy-router has been produced. However, rapid progress is being made, and products with partial functions are continuously being introduced.

ENN Group has been dedicated to promoting the concept of the Universal Energy Network for over a decade, and its concept aligns closely with the connotation of the Energy Internet (Figure 2-14). Its demonstration project, the Sino-German Ecopark, is located in Qingdao, Shandong Province. It is one of China's first batch of multi-energy complementary integrated optimization demonstration projects and new energy microgrid demonstration projects. Covering a planned area of 11.59 square kilometers, the project encompasses various sectors such as industry, commerce, and residences. ENN has broken away from traditional separate energy planning models and conducted universal energy planning in close integration with urban planning to achieve an overall optimized layout of load-source-network-storage. Firstly, it optimizes the demand side by integrating technologies such as bionic ventilation and building energy efficiency to develop green buildings and reduce energy consumption. Secondly, it promotes multi-energy complementarity and multi-technology integration, fully utilizing local solar, geothermal, biomass, and waste energy, combined with energy storage technologies, to support clean, low-carbon, and efficient energy conversion. Thirdly, it dynamically reconstructs supply and demand to match the park's short-, medium-, and long-term load growth. In the short to medium term, appropriately sized universal energy stations are constructed based on load conditions. In the long term, various energy facilities are interconnected and collaborate to supply energy, building a park-wide universal energy network. The universal energy network operation, scheduling, and trading platform is utilized for overall optimization and matching, reducing investment and energy consumption costs, and supporting the efficient operation of the park's universal energy network. Two universal energy stations have been completed and put into operation and are now interconnected. Upon full completion of the project, the overall energy utilization efficiency is expected to exceed 80%, with renewable energy utilization reaching over 20%.

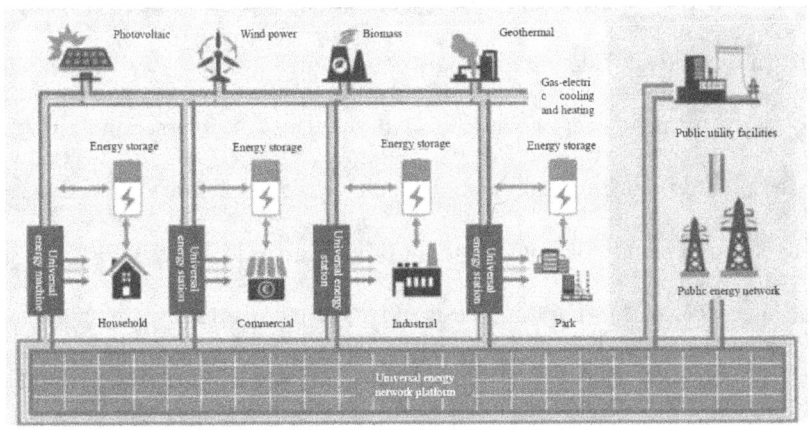

Figure 2-14 Schematic Diagram of ENANET (Ubiquitous Energy Network) of ENN Group

Note: The ENANET integrates information networks with energy infrastructure and loads. By utilizing big data and intelligent control systems, it enhances efficiency and optimizes system operation. This represents an initial practice of the energy internet.

The Ubiquitous Power Internet of Things (UPIoT) is a manifestation of the Energy Internet concept within the power grid. State Grid Corporation of China (SGCC) is making comprehensive deployments for the construction of the UPIoT, aiming to initially establish it by 2021. This will involve achieving basic business collaboration and data connectivity, preliminary unified IoT management, and support for the development of both grid and emerging businesses.

Against the backdrop of an increasing proportion of new energy grid connections and the continuous deepening of power sector reforms, traditional power grids and enterprises face greater external competitive pressures. Meanwhile, traditional equipment struggles to match the volatility of new energy sources, and the lack of interaction with the external environment makes it difficult for enterprises to meet users' increasing demands. The integration of the smart grid and the UPIoT is an indispensable part of building the Energy Internet. Currently, China's smart grid has been developed for over a decade and is fully equipped to support the construction of the UPIoT, which SGCC has prioritized for the present and future.

The UPIoT is a smart service system that enables universal interconnection and human-machine interaction across all aspects of the power system by fully applying modern information technologies, such as mobile internet, artificial intelligence, and advanced communication technologies. It features comprehensive state perception, efficient information processing, and flexible application, and consists of four layers: the perception layer, network layer, platform layer, and application layer.

As a smart service system that achieves universal interconnection and human-machine interaction across all aspects of the power system, with features such as comprehensive state perception, the UPIoT is being uniformly promoted at the SGCC level and is expected to accelerate the business expansion of relevant enterprises. The UPIoT involves five levels: terminal information collectors (sensors, RFID, etc.), edge computing, communication networks, cloud platforms, and artificial intelligence. As investment in the UPIoT accelerates, it will bring business opportunities to enterprises across related industrial chains.

The Energy Internet encompasses not only the power grid but the entire energy system. Energy Ville, a renowned institution at the University of Leuven in Belgium dedicated to renewable energy and smart energy technology research, has made significant achievements in energy-efficient buildings, smart grids, and smart cities. Energy Ville has also developed a series of products and tools to support energy system decision-making and planning, applicable from individual buildings, neighborhoods, and cities to regional levels. Based on the Internet, these tools support energy transition path selection at multiple levels by calculating energy consumption, carbon dioxide emissions, and financing conditions, and combining the application of energy technologies and innovations such as district heating, cooling, and distributed renewable energy sources to provide holistic energy solutions. Its concepts and technologies are gaining increasing practical application in Europe.

The core of the Energy Internet is the integration of information and energy, aiming to achieve higher levels of energy efficiency and renewable energy utilization through a sharing philosophy. From this perspective, the development of the Energy Internet has already begun, although it has not yet reached a tipping point for explosive growth. As this tipping point approaches, the Energy Internet will redraw the landscape of our energy future.

Energy Services

Energy services have increasingly become a catchphrase emphasized by energy companies, with many traditional energy enterprises now identifying themselves as service providers. This reflects a shift in values: service creates more value. Initially, energy service companies were often synonymous with energy conservation firms. However, with the digital transformation reshaping the energy sector, energy services have evolved into a more universal concept. Many traditional energy companies, including giants like State Grid Corporation of China, are striving to transition into energy service enterprises. In the energy field, this transition carries substantial implications: service means not just supplying more energy but delivering it more efficiently.

Benoit Lebot, Secretary-General of the International Partnership for Energy Efficiency Cooperation, once shared a telling example. In traditional lighting, from coal mining, power generation, transmission, and distribution to the incandescent bulb, each stage incurs varying degrees of energy efficiency losses. Ultimately, less than 2% of the initially extracted energy is used to produce visible light, meaning the vast majority of energy is wasted.

Energy-saving technologies have advanced significantly over the years. For instance, in lighting, traditional incandescent bulbs waste most of their energy through filament heating. Energy-efficient bulbs improve efficiency by about five times, while LEDs further enhance energy efficiency, utilizing most of the energy for lighting. This demonstrates that improvements in end-use energy technologies can significantly conserve energy.

While energy conservation at critical stages is crucial, considering the entire energy chain, repeated energy conversions imply energy consumption, and the potential for further energy savings remains substantial, with digital technology playing a pivotal role.

Vertuoz, a subsidiary of France's ENGIE, established a digital platform for building energy management in 2012 and has since served over 15,000 buildings. By installing temperature, light, and carbon dioxide sensors in buildings, it collects energy consumption data. Its dynamic interface allows users to monitor and manage real-time energy consumption data. Based on data monitoring and analysis, it can generate energy consumption reports, set up abnormal energy consumption alerts, compare energy usage with similar users, collaborate with owners to develop energy-saving plans, and optimize building energy usage in real-time through remote intelligent energy efficiency monitoring and control systems.

In 2016, ENGIE signed a contract with the Paris municipal government to provide energy management services for 140 primary schools. By inspecting and improving building insulation, adopting more energy-efficient LEDs and boilers, and, most importantly, installing 6,800 remotely controllable thermostatic valves, the project achieved a 30% energy savings after two years, receiving positive evaluations.

ENGIE's example exemplifies energy services, leveraging digital technology for smarter management that matches energy supply with user demand in real-time, reducing unnecessary waste. With flexible market signals, it can also choose more economical energy sources, such as electricity, gas, or energy storage. In a green and low-carbon context, many clients demand tracking the carbon footprint of energy supply, and intelligent systems can help select greener energy sources.

In energy conservation, a precise understanding of energy consumption across different industries through digitalization is a prerequisite for energy savings. For instance, reducing energy consumption in wastewater treatment holds global significance, as wastewater treatment facilities typically consume over 25% of municipal electricity. The world's first energy-neutral/energy-producing water recycling project in Marselisborg, Aarhus, Denmark, is a prime example. Since 2010, Danfoss has collaborated with Aarhus to achieve intelligent water treatment, establish a smart model, and reduce energy consumption, testing and developing new technologies. By utilizing more sensors, advanced computer control, and sufficient frequency converters or variable-speed drives to optimize processes, the Marselisborg Wastewater Treatment Plant reduced energy consumption by 40%-50%.

Simultaneously, by adopting systematic solutions, the Marselisborg plant generates energy from organic waste like sludge, converting it into biogas for energy or fuel, and establishing a sustainable 24-hour management model. The plant not only minimizes energy consumption but also maximizes net energy surplus. Today, it not only reduces energy consumption but also supplies electricity and heating to Aarhus, Denmark's second-largest city. In 2016, the project produced 150% of its own electricity consumption and approximately 2.5 gigawatt-hours of surplus heat, with a total energy production of about 230% of its own energy consumption. Water leakage rates dropped to 6%, and water prices decreased by 9%. Recognized as an advanced case in wastewater treatment by the International Energy Agency, the project contributed to a 35% reduction in Aarhus's carbon footprint. The wastewater treatment plant has transformed from a high-energy consumer to an energy supplier, becoming a typical energy prosumer. The Marselisborg case demonstrates the immense potential for industrial users to become energy prosumers with digital technology support. In recent years, many factory roofs in China have been equipped with solar panels, enabling self-sufficient energy production and consumption.

British company Grid Edge developed an AI system called Flex2X, utilizing machine learning algorithms for building energy management. By accessing vast amounts of historical data and external data (e.g., weather forecasts), it manages building energy consumption in real-time. Dubbed "artificial intelligence," the system learns from received data and makes corresponding adjustments. Based on past learning experiences, it can predict building energy consumption 24 hours in advance.

Connected to smart meters and the power distribution network, the software system monitors electricity prices and sources, enabling it to increase or decrease building power loads at any time based on cost or carbon intensity (Figure 2-15).

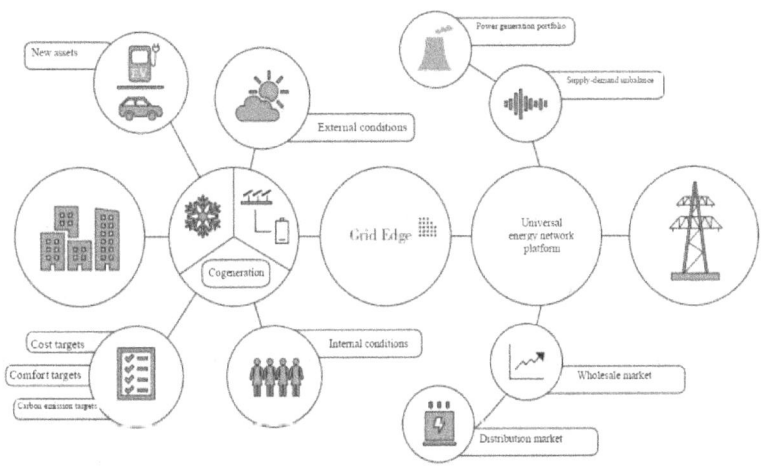

Figure 2-15 Schematic Diagram of the Grid Edge Intelligent Software

System (Courtesy of Grid Edge)

Note: It connects energy-consuming entities with energy supply systems, and this digital, flexible response provides better tools for systematically improving energy efficiency.

By controlling building energy consumption, the digital system transforms the building's energy consumption pattern from fixed to flexible, which holds high commercial value in the current power grid system. Flexible loads support system peak-shaving management, enabling more renewable energy integration and reducing wind and solar curtailment. Digitalization of energy-consuming terminals lays the foundation for systematically improving energy efficiency.

Danish company Danfoss developed an AI algorithm called Leanheat for regional energy systems. This system provides optimal secondary water outlet operation strategies for heat exchange stations based on future meteorological trends, maximizing energy savings and improving energy transmission and distribution efficiency while meeting indoor temperature requirements. Leanheat is an intelligent software control platform based on real-time indoor temperature monitoring and heat exchange station control, aimed at energy conservation, emission reduction, and improving heating quality for users. Its core control principle is as follows (Figure 2-16).

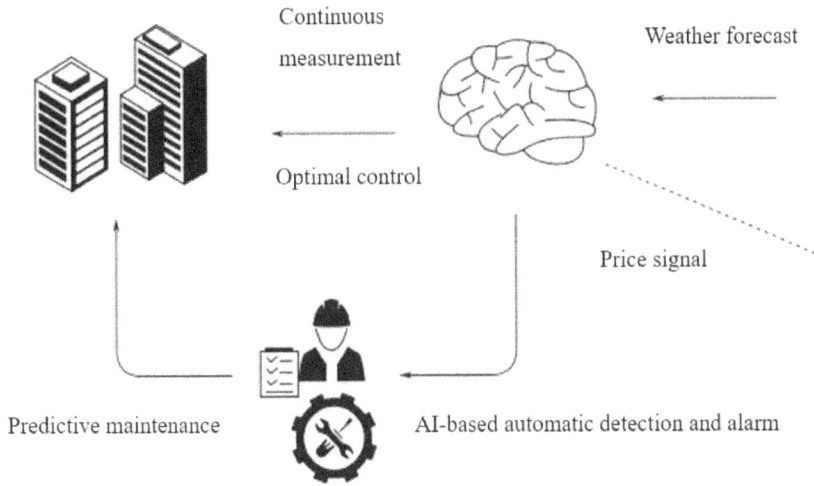

Figure 2-16 Schematic Diagram of the Operating Principle of Danfoss's

Leanheat System (Source: Danfoss)

As shown in the figure, based on outdoor temperature forecasts, it provides real-time secondary water supply temperature setpoints for heat exchange stations. By continuously monitoring operational parameters of heat exchange stations and real-time indoor temperatures of users (all or part), it utilizes AI and self-learning methods to optimize secondary water supply temperature targets, ensuring the lowest possible secondary water supply temperature meets indoor temperature requirements for users. Meanwhile, with AI assistance, it automatically tracks the operational status of heat exchange station equipment, enhancing operational safety and reliability.

Germany's Next-Kraftwerke has become one of Europe's largest virtual power plant operators without owning any power stations, with operations spanning Germany, Belgium, and other European countries. As an EPEX-certified trader, it participates in the energy spot market, managing over 4,200 distributed generation and energy storage devices, including biomass power plants, combined heat and power, hydroelectric stations, wind and solar photovoltaic power plants, and controllable loads, with a total management capacity exceeding 2.8 million kilowatts, a figure that continues to grow.

The company's core product is the remote control device NextBox, installed on volatile power generation facilities like wind and solar power. Through its virtual power plant platform, it manages controlled power sources, participates in power market trading, and shares profits. With its data capabilities, Next-Kraftwerke also leverages the fast startup and flexible output characteristics of biomass power and hydropower to participate in secondary and tertiary frequency regulation of the power grid, earning additional revenue and accounting for 10% of Germany's secondary frequency regulation market.

To enhance flexibility, Next-Kraftwerke introduced standardized energy storage modules, including a 2-megawatt container connected to the grid via "NextBox." The company uses software to integrate power sources and energy storage onto its management platform, jointly providing ancillary services, enabling efficient and profitable operations. This energy

storage container with equipment already possesses the functions of an
energy router envisioned in the energy internet concept (Figure 2-17).

Figure 2-17 Schematic Diagram of NextBox and Related Systems

(Source: Next-Kraftwerke)

Next-Kraftwerke's core product is not energy but data. By collecting
data through NextBox, it decides when and how to supply electricity.
Through this management capability, the company profits while
significantly reducing the need for backup power plants and avoiding
investment waste. This can be seen as a broad improvement in energy
efficiency, where enhancing the utilization efficiency of energy facilities
can reduce resource waste more effectively than mere energy conservation.

At the national level, digitalization is equally crucial for energy management. Australia provides an excellent example, demonstrating that improved national-level energy digitalization enhances governance capabilities and aids in formulating more precise and effective energy policies (Figure 2-18).

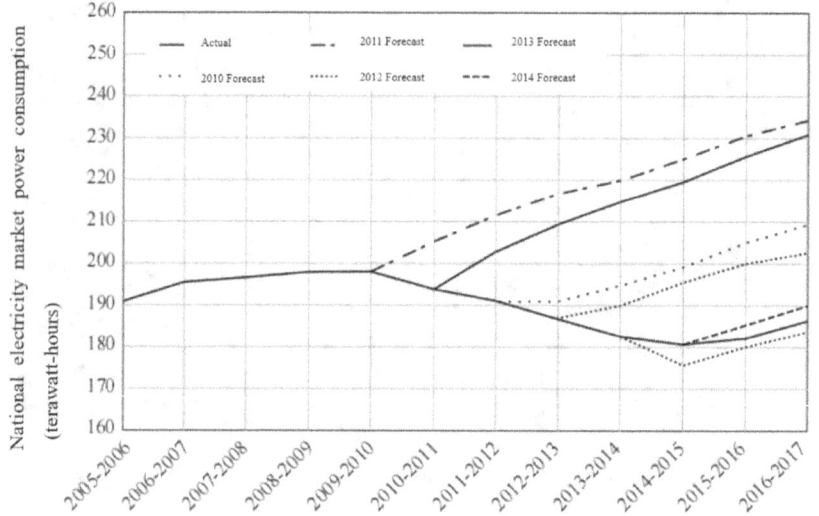

Figure 2-18 Schematic Diagram Comparing Electricity Consumption

Forecasts with Actual Conditions in Australia

(Source: Australian Department of the Environment and Energy)

The light-colored line in the figure represents Australia's projected electricity consumption curve in recent years, while the black solid line represents actual consumption. For years, due to a lack of in-depth analysis of consumption-side data, Australian government departments have experienced significant discrepancies between projected and actual electricity consumption, with actual consumption consistently falling far below projections. Based on such data and forecasting capabilities, it is challenging to achieve policy goals as expected.

To enhance energy data analysis capabilities and improve the precision of energy planning and policy formulation, the Australian government invested 20 million Australian dollars in launching the National Energy Data Analysis Research (NEAR) program. This program is implemented by government departments, science and industry associations, and the Australian Energy Market Operator. As a crucial component of the project, it further acquired consumption-side energy data, including industrial, commercial, and residential energy consumption, encompassing factors such as appliance usage, building characteristics, population distribution, consumption habits, and economic structural changes. The project team focused on analyzing the impact of air conditioning and rooftop solar photovoltaics, two critical factors affecting electricity consumption, deepening the understanding of energy consumption trends. Due to relatively high electricity prices in Australia, rooftop solar photovoltaics are highly competitive and have developed rapidly. These data analyses provide a reliable basis for formulating targeted policy measures, such as energy efficiency standards and grid access services.

As people often prioritize energy production over energy efficiency, Fatih Birol, the newly appointed Executive Director of the International

Energy Agency, has prominently raised the banner of energy efficiency, declaring that the cleanest energy is the energy saved. Even clean solar energy has environmental impacts during manufacturing and other stages. Energy efficiency improvements result in minimal negative environmental impacts.

This is not just a slogan but can be specifically quantified. According to the International Energy Agency's annual energy efficiency reports, the potential of energy efficiency is vastly underestimated by the public. Based on the International Energy Agency's calculations, to achieve the temperature control goals of *the Paris Agreement*, the potential contribution of energy efficiency exceeds the total contribution of renewable energy sources. Therefore, placing high importance on energy efficiency is entirely justified (Figure 2-19).

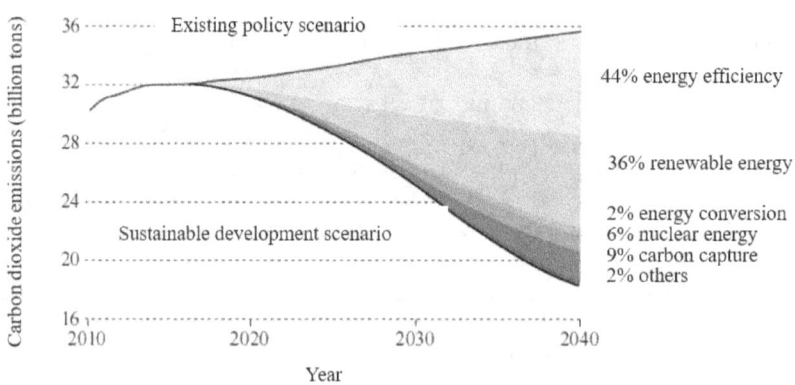

Figure 2-19 Schematic Diagram of Emission Reduction Contributions

from Various Measures (Source: IEA)

Note: From this projection by the IEA on achieving sustainable development by 2040, it can be seen that energy efficiency contributions are the most significant factor.

Traditionally, the segmentation of different energy categories has hindered their comprehensive utilization and efficient substitution potential. With improved digital capabilities, energy service companies can optimize energy supply methods and sources more effectively, systematically enhancing energy efficiency levels. However, for traditional energy companies, this is almost unfamiliar territory. Whether the energy services slogan can be effectively implemented is a litmus test for energy company transformation and a key to upgrading national energy strategies.

Part III

The Invisible Hand of Finance

Energy has always been closely linked to finance, not only because it is a capital-intensive industry but also because finance is actively influencing energy development. In the future, blockchain technology will forge new energy currencies, a trend already emerging.

The relationship between modern energy and finance is inseparable. As the largest-scale traded product globally, energy serves as a crucial underpinning for various financial derivatives. Meanwhile, the dollar-denomination of major energy commodities such as oil and natural gas has effectively upheld the US dollar's status as the world's reserve currency. If technological progress has heralded the dawn of an energy revolution, then finance stands as a potent driving force behind it. However, such financial support may not primarily stem from efforts to address climate change or promote human well-being, but rather from the pursuit of higher returns. With the application of blockchain technology in both the financial and energy sectors, a new integration of energy and finance is on the horizon, poised to profoundly reshape the landscapes of both industries.

Petrodollar and Energy Finance

In July 1944, representatives from 44 countries convened the renowned Bretton Woods Conference in Bretton Woods, New Hampshire, USA, announcing the establishment of two major institutions—the International Bank for Reconstruction and Development (the precursor to the World Bank) and the International Monetary Fund (IMF)—and reaching the *Agreement of the International Monetary Fund*. This agreement established the dominance of the US dollar in the international monetary system and laid the foundation for a new post-war international monetary order. Participating countries agreed to establish an international monetary system managed by the newly formed IMF and its auxiliary institution, the International Bank for Reconstruction and Development, to maintain stable international exchange rates, multilateral trade, and currency convertibility. The IMF Agreement set the official price of gold at $35 per ounce.

During the 1960s and 1970s, the United States became mired in the Vietnam War, resulting in significant fiscal deficits and a deterioration in its international income situation, triggering multiple dollar crises. The large-scale repurchase of gold held in the United States by concerned countries exacerbated these crises. In August 1971, the Nixon administration unilaterally announced the abandonment of the "gold standard" and implemented a free-floating exchange rate between gold and the dollar, leading to the collapse of the Bretton Woods monetary system.

However, the World Bank and the IMF continued to exist. The US dollar, now decoupled from gold, relied on the geopolitical strength of the United States for support. President Nixon agreed to provide military armaments and protection to Saudi Arabia on the condition that all Saudi oil transactions be settled in US dollars, thereby bolstering the dollar's international status. As Saudi Arabia was the largest oil producer within OPEC and the world's largest oil exporter, other countries soon adopted the US dollar for oil transactions, thus establishing the petrodollar system.

Although the US dollar could no longer stably purchase gold, it could reliably buy oil, a far more valuable and indispensable strategic resource for modern nations. Consequently, many countries continued to use the US dollar as their primary foreign exchange reserve, maintaining its status as the world's reserve currency. The relationship between finance and energy was elevated to a new strategic level.

Entering the new century, the US dollar, or rather finance, gave birth to another massive energy industry—shale oil and gas. This time, financial markets played a more proactive role, with the shale oil and gas revolution occurring under the auspices of financial investment. In his dedicated research on shale oil, Deng Zhenghong compared a series of data and concluded that shale oil and gas production is closely linked to Federal Reserve policies.

In 2019, US shale oil production reached a record high of 7 million barrels per day, surpassing Saudi Arabia to become the world's largest oil producer. It is projected that the United States will become a net oil exporter within two years, a scenario that was almost unimaginable just five years ago. In 2018, US shale gas production once again achieved double-digit growth, exceeding 830 billion cubic meters and far outpacing Russia, which ranked second.

The successful development of shale oil and gas in the United States has profoundly altered the global energy supply and demand landscape, as well as geopolitical relations, enabling the United States to achieve its long-held dream of "energy independence" by reducing its dependence on energy imports. With a significant decline in US energy prices, natural gas-fired power generation has become cheaper than coal-fired generation, resulting in substantially lower electricity prices in the United States compared to many other countries worldwide, particularly for industrial users, including developing nations like China. This has injected new vitality into the US manufacturing sector. For instance, one of the primary considerations for Fuyao Glass, a Chinese company, in establishing a factory in the United States was the low energy costs. Low-cost natural gas has not only enhanced the economic competitiveness of the United States but also significantly reduced carbon dioxide emissions, exerting a profound impact on the global economy. In this regard, the shale oil and gas revolution and the new energy revolution complement each other, sharing the important similarity of being driven by energy finance.

In June 2010, at the Global Unconventional Gas Conference held in Amsterdam, 91-year-old Mitchell was awarded the Lifetime Achievement Award by the Gas Technology Institute (GTI) and was hailed as the father of US shale gas. Since 1981, Mitchell and his company, Mitchell Energy & Development Corp., spent 17 years searching for methods to extract shale gas from rock formations, testing various drilling and fracturing techniques. It was not until 1998 that they began large-scale and economically viable shale gas development, laying the foundation for the US shale gas revolution.

Mitchell was not alone in this endeavor. During the same period, numerous small and medium-sized enterprises explored shale oil and gas development, including well-known companies like Chesapeake and EOG. These companies, considered challengers to the traditional oil and gas industry, adopted vastly different approaches. Due to their limited financial resources, they relied heavily on external funding. From the outset, shale oil and gas development exhibited strong capital operation and financial characteristics. These early shale oil and gas developers often sought investor funding on the same day they leased oil and gas blocks. During the 2014 oil price plunge, financial institutions developed various hedging, equity transfer, and financial product bundling strategies to help these shale oil and gas companies raise funds and maintain cash flow, preventing bankruptcies due to capital chain disruptions. These venture capital firms and funds supporting shale oil and gas development were often also investors in new energy.

US shale oil production maintained rapid growth for a decade, with annual production increases exceeding 50 million tons in multiple years, equivalent to adding the output of a Daqing Oilfield annually—an unprecedented feat in the history of the global oil industry (Figure 3-1).

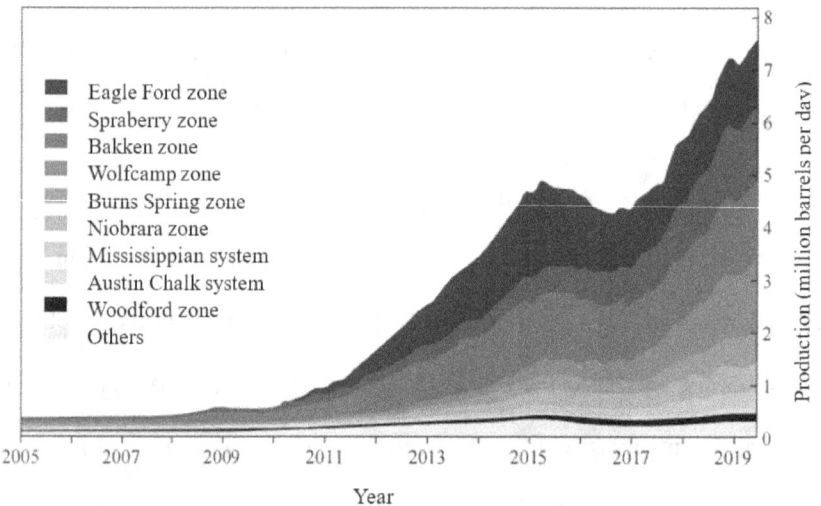

Figure 3-1 Growth Curve of U.S. Shale Oil Production (Source: U.S. Energy Information Administration)

After years of negative cash flow and continuous investment, the shale oil industry finally achieved positive overall cash flow in 2018 (Figure 3-2). Throughout the lengthy research and investment history of shale oil, questions have persistently arisen regarding the sustainability of this model. How could an industry rely on continuous losses for development? Some even questioned whether it was a "Ponzi scheme." Such skepticism often originated from traditional industries. However, when considering the investment models in the information and internet industries and the new energy sector, this approach is not uncommon. For example, JD.com only achieved profitability after more than a decade of losses. During this extended investment period, despite the lack of profits, investors focused more on rapid revenue growth, indicating greater future profitability—a similarity shared with the shale oil and gas industry.

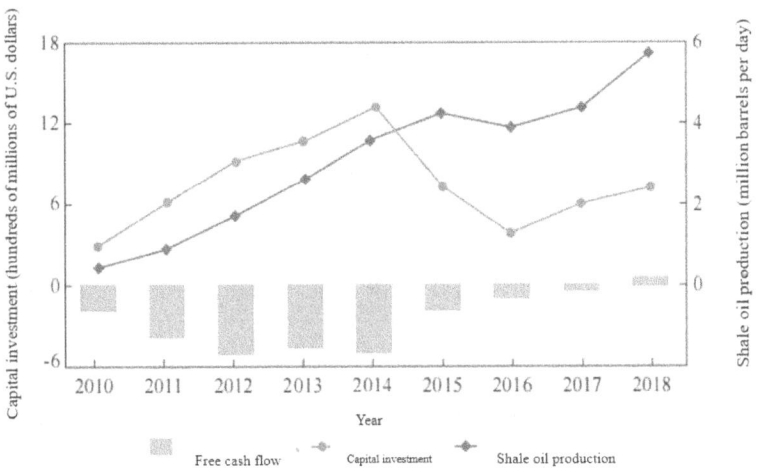

Figure 3-2 Historical Capital Expenditure Trends in the U.S. Shale Oil Industry (Source: IEA)

In recent years, green finance has emerged as a buzzword, with the international community hoping to leverage financial and investment tools to promote low-carbon energy transitions, achieve energy conservation, emission reduction, and sustainable development. Finance is increasingly taking a proactive role in shaping the direction of energy development.

The Rocky Mountain Institute provides a typical case of green finance. Inspired by municipal infrastructure financing, Berkeley, California, established a green financing mechanism called Property Assessed Clean Energy (PACE).

This mechanism enables property owners to obtain upfront investment for energy efficiency projects from third-party investors, covering all costs associated with energy efficiency upgrades, such as installing rooftop solar panels, upgrading heating and cooling systems, renovating water pumps, and enhancing building envelopes. Investors coordinate with local tax authorities to add additional repayment items to property tax bills, specifying the repayment amount per period and the total repayment duration. For property owners, this means they can enjoy low-cost specialized loans without going through cumbersome application processes, along with subsequent energy cost savings and improved comfort from energy efficiency upgrades.

PACE has broken through barriers to the development of the energy efficiency market. By linking to property taxes, it effectively mobilizes social capital investment in energy efficiency and new energy applications, reducing government fiscal pressure. The US Environmental Protection

Agency provided Berkeley with a grant to support the preparation of the *Local Government Guide to Energy Efficiency Improvement and Renewable Energy Use*. PACE received official support from the White House in 2009, and its adoption rate has since soared. To date, over 32 US states have passed PACE legislation, covering more than 80% of the population (Figure 3-3).

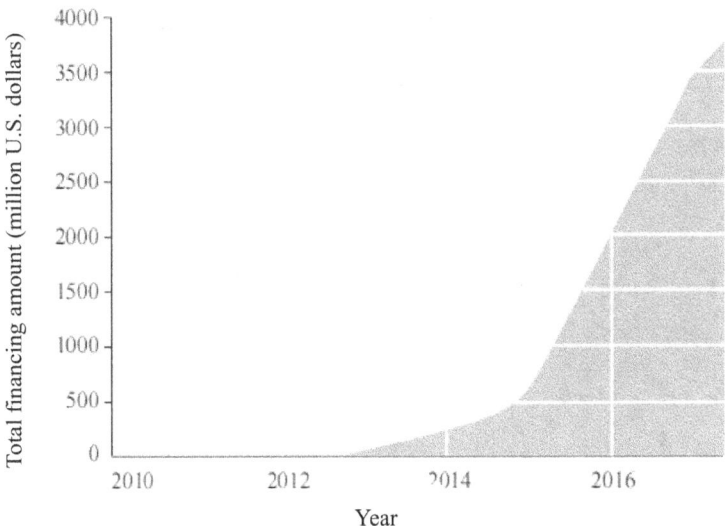

Figure 3-3 Growth of PACE Financing Volume for Residential Buildings in the United States (Source: Financial Magazine)

Investment targets the future, especially for emerging industries with unclear prospects. This is why the investment sector may be more sensitive than the energy industry in these areas. If finance is increasingly shaping the trajectory of energy development, the success of shale oil and gas and green finance is just the beginning.

New Practices in Energy Trading

In the spring of 2016, April 12th fell on a Monday. Under the operation of LO3 Energy, TransActive Grid established a microgrid in the Brooklyn district. However, this microgrid differed from traditional ones as it aimed to create a brand-new business model through blockchain technology. Within this network, peer-to-peer personal energy trading was realized, and a new financial settlement model was adopted. Lawrence Orsini, the co-founder, stated that this was a momentous occasion to be remembered in the energy industry (Figure 3-4).

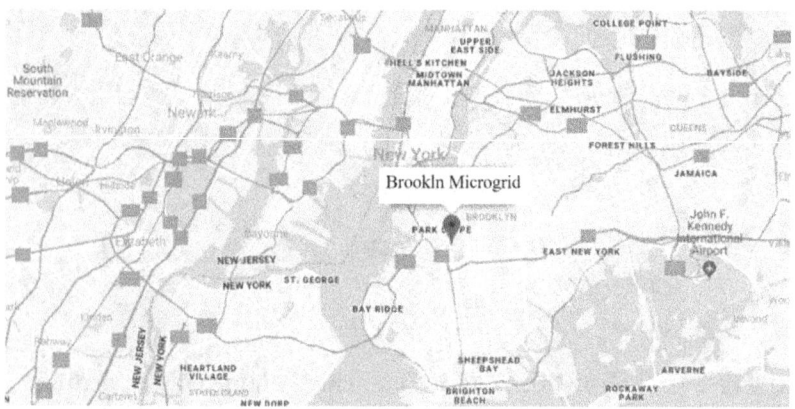

Figure 3-4 Location Map of Brooklyn Microgrid

Note: The Brooklyn neighborhood, situated within the Park Slope and Gowanus residential communities in eastern New York, is at the forefront of innovative distributed energy trading, which may potentially pioneer a new energy model.

As a pioneer, this project excelled at engaging the public and frequently organized professional or public seminars. On the project's dedicated website, its vision and mission were clearly conveyed: to increase the production of local clean and renewable energy; to develop an energy internet that connects distributed energy sources, enhancing the reliability and efficiency of the power grid; and to create financial incentives and business models to encourage community investment in local renewable energy.

These three aspects seemed to have perfectly fulfilled Rifkin's vision in *The Third Industrial Revolution* regarding the coupling of information and renewable energy. Rifkin's prediction appeared to be coming true even faster than expected, as the implementation of this project took place just over four years after the publication of his book.

Looking up at the sky above Brooklyn, rooftop photovoltaic systems had become ubiquitous (Figure 3-5). Among all local energy resources, PV remained the primary source due to its wide adaptability, relatively low investment, and simple technical implementation. Other local energy sources such as biomass (waste), geothermal energy, and wind power faced more constraints.

Figure 3-5 Aerial View of Brooklyn

Note: The local energy in Brooklyn mainly comes from solar ph otovoltaic systems. More importantly, it has initiated a new energy tra ding model, heralding a novel energy landscape. Image source: https:// www.brooklyn.energy/

The Brooklyn energy microgrid interaction encompassed both demand and supply aspects. A dedicated interactive webpage was set up, and the Brooklyn project provided a platform for direct trading of renewable energy, with one-stop services available behind the platform. When customers made choices, they not only knew where the energy came from but also could deeply participate in the process. The platform operated on smart contracts based on Ethereum, developed by Tendermint. During transactions, energy virtual currency was generated, which could be used within the microgrid according to the contract. Through blockchain technology, the virtual currency could be produced along with PV power generation and transferred between the electronic wallets of producers and consumers. When consumers consumed electricity, the virtual currency would be automatically deducted from their wallets.

Both sellers and consumers could submit specific price requests to the platform, and prices would automatically interact and generate real-time prices on the platform, with a new price cleared every 15 minutes. Transactions were immediately recorded in the distributed ledger, and both transactions and payments were automatically executed according to smart contracts. Users could flexibly set their preferences, such as the proportion of green energy and the amount of local energy they wanted, and could even prioritize purchasing electricity generated by their friends' homes.

Energy suddenly became accessible and was accompanied by considerate services, an experience that traditional energy companies could not offer. As various industries were emphasizing customization and user experience, the energy industry in Brooklyn finally ushered in a new dawn.

This customization and user experience were based on Internet connectivity and a new business model, including new trading currencies, representing a comprehensive attempt at energy Internetization. The number of participants had rapidly grown from a dozen initially to several hundred. By the end of 2017, the project had approximately 50 prosumers and 500 consumers. However, the project also encountered many challenges during its advancement. As the frequency of transactions increased, blockchain technology urgently needed improvement in supporting high-performance and low-cost power trading. Later, as the scale expanded, the New York government required prosumers in the pilot project to pay taxes, significantly increasing costs. LO3 Energy, the project operator, also began seeking new project opportunities in other countries and regions. The replicability of this model would soon become more evident, potentially revolutionizing the structure of the energy industry.

In Germany, energy storage companies were also engaging in similar business model innovations. Europe's major grid company, TenneT, collaborated with the energy storage company Sonnen to network decentralized home energy storage batteries. After a year and a half of pilot testing, they achieved excellent results and believed that this model had broad prospects (Figure 3-6).

Figure 3-6 Standardized Products of Sonnen Company

Note: Standardized products facilitate Sonnen's promotion of its energy storage modules, with complex systems hidden behind the simplicity of the products. (Image source: Sonnen Company)

Sonnen was a company dedicated to home energy storage. As of then, it had approximately 40,000 home energy storage systems in Europe, each with a storage capacity ranging from 5 kilowatt-hours to 15 kilowatt-hours. This overall network system was similar to a "virtual power plant," with a total capacity of about 400 megawatt-hours, and its peak shaving and frequency regulation performance was comparable to that of backup installed capacity in the millions of kilowatts. The Sonnen system had obtained first-level energy storage qualification from the EU, enabling direct connection to the grid.

Sonnen's home energy storage systems were mainly used in conjunction with distributed home PV and wind power systems. Notably, through Sonnen's Flat-Box system, hundreds or thousands of decentralized energy storage systems were interconnected, meaning that users could not only obtain electricity from their own energy storage systems but could also supply power to each other through this network. This virtual "energy storage pool" ensured a stable power supply under most conditions (Figure 3-7). Behind this system was the support of the Internet and big data, which provided real-time information on the remaining power and allocable resources of each energy storage system.

Consumed stored energy   Consumed solar energy   Solar energy production

Figure 3-7 Schematic Diagram of Energy Storage and Photovoltaic

Matching

Note: Household electricity consumption peaks in the morning and evening, while the peak generation period for photovoltaic power is at noon. The stored energy can not only be used by households but also contribute to grid peak shaving. (Image source: Sonnen)

According to Sonnen's introduction, joining its home energy storage system not only allowed users to utilize green energy but also offered economic benefits. If users agreed to connect to the system and provide peak shaving power during peak hours (perhaps just for a few minutes a day, barely noticeable), they could enjoy a zero electricity rate, meaning that all the electricity consumption specified in their contracts would be free. The membership fee for joining this network was €19.99 per month, but it significantly reduced electricity bills compared to the original basic electricity charges (the average monthly electricity bill for a European household was around €50).

It was worth mentioning that the far-sighted Chinese private enterprise Envision Energy became one of the two new shareholders of Sonnen during its $85 million funding round in October 2016. In February 2019, the international energy giant Shell decided to fully acquire Sonnen. Shell's new energy company was fully committed to deploying new energy in Europe, and this partnership opened up greater possibilities for the future.

The pilot project between Sonnen and TenneT was located in some areas of northern and southern Germany. In addition to Sonnen's home energy storage system network, it was equipped with an intelligent charging management system and a super-distributed ledger system based on blockchain technology. This ledger system was an open-source blockchain platform developed by IBM that enabled smart contract functionality. Experts explained that it could be regarded as an operating system for markets, decentralized data-sharing networks, and cryptocurrencies, significantly reducing the costs and complexity involved in energy trading.

During the pilot, Sonnen used a blockchain solution to specify the combined capacity that could be provided from home battery systems to TenneT at specific times for rescheduling. Each time Sonnen sent data, it was recorded as an automatically generated "quote" in the distributed ledger. If TenneT accepted the quote, batteries in areas with surplus energy (e.g., where there was strong wind) would be automatically charged and would release power to the grid as needed. The real-time documentation in the distributed ledger meant that "every kilowatt-hour of electricity traded—whether stored or discharged—would generate a unique and transparent encrypted signature that could be used for settlement."

According to TenneT and Sonnen, the pilot demonstrated how energy storage systems, including car batteries, could effectively use blockchain to provide stability services to the grid. One of the main advantages of this technology was that it established a tamper-proof system where millions of transactions were automated and could be executed at very low transaction costs. This decentralized data exchange ensured that individual units could flexibly align with the grid system's demands.

TenneT stated that this pilot was one of many initiatives aimed at addressing the challenges posed by the energy transition to the grid by 2030. As the share of renewable energy continued to grow, so did the volatility on the demand side. René Kerkmeester, TenneT's Head of Digital Transformation, said, "For example, we know there are electric vehicles that need charging, but we don't know exactly when and where. The cost of rescheduling due to grid congestion and capacity constraints, which is usually passed on to consumers, is close to €1 billion per year. New technologies can significantly reduce this cost."

Of course, even if the demonstration projects were successful, these innovations required more external conditions for large-scale promotion. Even in Western countries with well-developed market conditions, these business model innovations faced numerous challenges, with the most crucial being the need for changes in the policy environment.

Blockchain's Reach in Energy

As discussed in other chapters of this book, blockchain technology is making its mark in the energy sector, with some applications already standing out. The prospects for blockchain in the energy industry are as promising as those in the financial sector, as this technology can ensure open and timely exchanges of energy value, enhancing trust between consumers and suppliers. These solutions will effectively reduce transaction costs, improve efficiency, intensify competition among service providers, and further drive down service costs.

As shown in the figure below, according to Venture Scanner data, global funding for blockchain-related technology companies reached a record $4.1 billion in 2018, up 28% from the previous year. Over the past five years, the compound annual growth rate of blockchain investments has been 87%. Few emerging industries have received such strong support from capital markets, indicating that blockchain's grand future across various industries is just beginning (Figure 3-8).

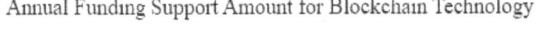

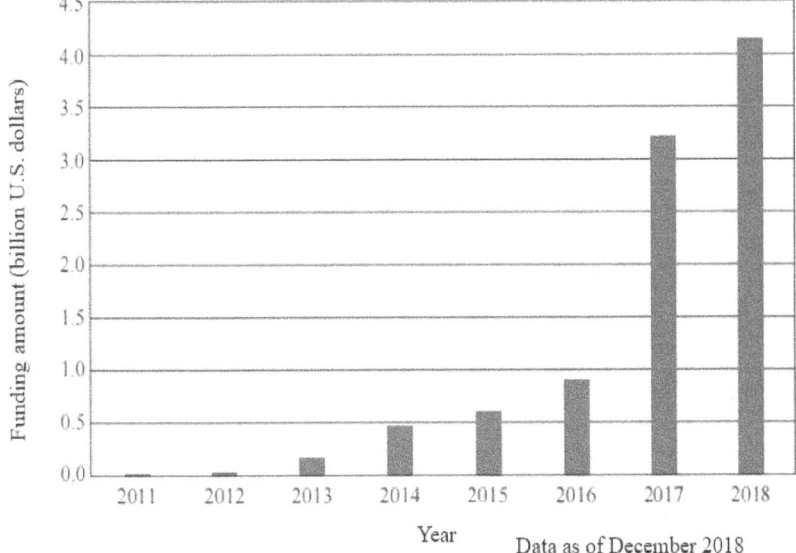

Figure 3-8 Growth in Funding Received by Blockchain Technology

Companies (Source: Venture Scanner)

To better understand the impact of finance in the energy sector, it is essential to first understand the technology of "blockchain." On October 24, 2019, President Xi Jinping led a special collective study session on blockchain with the Political Bureau, which led to unprecedented attention to this technology in China.

On October 31, 2008, the Bitcoin white paper was released, and an enigmatic figure known as Satoshi Nakamoto, whose true identity remains unverified, opened the door to blockchain technology. Blockchain can be described as a special type of distributed database, also known as a distributed ledger. Its primary function is to store information; any information that needs to be preserved can be written into the blockchain and read from it. Its core technologies include distributed database technology, peer-to-peer networks, encryption algorithms, and consensus mechanisms. The encryption algorithms used to create blockchain ensure high credibility by recording blocks in chronological order, with block header information encrypted using hash algorithms. This combination of hash algorithms and timestamps ensures the temporal order and irreversible encryption of transaction data. Blockchain records each event and links it to the previous one, akin to adding new blocks to a chain, which is the origin of the term "blockchain" (Figure 3-9).

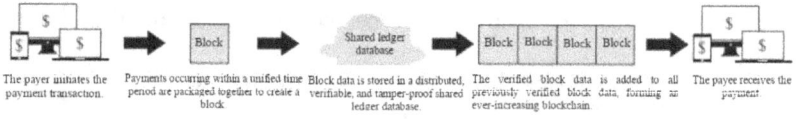

The payer initiates the payment transaction. Payments occurring within a unified time period are packaged together to create a block. Block data is stored in a distributed, verifiable, and tamper-proof shared ledger database. The verified block data is added to all previously verified block data, forming an ever-increasing blockchain. The payee receives the payment.

Figure 3-9 Schematic Diagram of Blockchain Transactions

Note: Transactions conducted on the blockchain do not require intermediaries or authoritative verification; they are automatically executed according to smart contracts.

This technical and somewhat convoluted explanation may still be difficult for those unfamiliar with blockchain to understand. To illustrate blockchain with a real-life example, consider how a production team leader in a village would announce each person's labor points over a loudspeaker every day. These labor points are akin to digital assets on a blockchain, and the daily announcement of point allocations is similar to broadcasting transactions on a blockchain. Everyone records this information, ensuring transparency and immutability. At the end of the month or a predetermined time, these points can be exchanged for grain or money. Although people in that era often complained about poverty, there were few complaints about fairness. In a sense, they had a primitive version of blockchain that helped establish a fair and transparent system, contributing to a more equitable society.

In this analogy, the production team leader still serves as a central authority. However, blockchain does not necessarily exclude central authorities. If the production team leader is democratically elected based on a mechanism agreed upon by everyone, and a new leader is elected for each announcement, this can still be considered a blockchain system. Such consensus mechanisms within blockchain are known as Proof of Stake, which is currently one of the most popular consensus mechanisms and serves as an effective channel for "returning power to the people."

Yu Yingjiao from Sinochem, who is dedicated to blockchain research and application, recommended another analogy that highlights the revolutionary impact of blockchain.

Consider how language evolved and continues to evolve. Who invented the Chinese language? For over 4,000 years, Chinese has developed, been transmitted, and evolved in a distributed manner without a central organizer. This distributed nature of language bears a strong resemblance to blockchain.

1.Immutability: Language is a historical legacy that cannot be altered. For example, to change the meaning and connotation of the phrase "wo xin chan dan" (to endure hardships for self-improvement), would we need to travel back to the Warring States period to modify history or have billions of Chinese speakers correct each other in person?

2.Consistency: Errors in language can become widely accepted over time. For instance, the phrase "wu du bu zhang fu" (often misinterpreted as "a man must be ruthless to succeed") originally meant "a man without magnanimity cannot be a true gentleman." Similarly, "ren bu wei ji, tian zhu di mie" (often misinterpreted as "if one does not act selfishly, heaven and earth will perish") actually means that "wei" refers to self-cultivation. If Mencius knew his words would be misused, he would surely be dismayed. Due to frequent misuse, these incorrect meanings have become widely accepted. New words and phrases continue to be added to the distributed database of human language, contributing to its richness and growth. The vast community of Chinese speakers actively contributes to the language's prosperity around the clock, across time and space.

3.Stability: Eradicating the Chinese language would require eliminating all its speakers, as each person carries a distributed server—their brain—containing a highly overlapping and identical database, ensuring robustness.

4.Forking Principle: Japanese and Korean, both written using Chinese characters, have diverged significantly in pronunciation and script. This is akin to a hard fork in blockchain, where consensus diverges due to geographical isolation or differing political views, resulting in distinct yet related languages.

These features encompass all the elements of blockchain. While comparing blockchain to language may seem to elevate its status and influence excessively, there is no doubt that this new technology will have a profound and far-reaching impact on the world.

A distributed ledger is a shared, synchronized database among network members that records transactions between participants, such as exchanges of assets or data. These assets can be tangible physical assets (e.g., land or gasoline) or intangible virtual assets (e.g., contracts, patents, and securities). In a mature market economy, exchanges create value by transferring ownership of assets within commercial networks. Traditional commercial ledgers have many shortcomings, including inefficiency, high costs, lack of transparency, and susceptibility to fraud and abuse. These issues necessitate support from authoritative or third-party institutions, which incur additional costs and introduce new opportunities for fraud and abuse. Even high-level authorities like governments are not immune to corruption. Credit is the core of finance, and traditional financial institutions primarily provide credit-based services. However, blockchain-driven distributed ledgers create new ways to establish credit.

Each record in a distributed ledger has a timestamp and a unique cryptographic signature, making the ledger an auditable history of all network transactions. Participants update records based on consensus principles. Anyone can join the blockchain network via the internet and become a node. In the blockchain world, there are no central nodes; each node is equal and stores the entire database. Data can be written to or read from any node, as all nodes eventually synchronize to ensure blockchain consistency.

Blockchain has no administrators and does not require audits, as its design aims to prevent centralized control. This lack of management ensures that blockchain cannot be controlled. If large corporations or governments gained control, they would dominate the platform, forcing other users to comply. Without the involvement of authoritative or intermediary third parties (e.g., financial institutions), creating universally accepted credit within distributed ledgers or blockchain is the core of this groundbreaking technology.

Blockchain expert Cao Yin argues that blockchain does not necessarily exclude centralization. There are three levels of decentralization in blockchain: architectural, governance, and logical.

1.Architectural Decentralization: How many physical computers compose the system, and how many can simultaneously fail without disrupting operations?

2.Governance Decentralization: How many individuals or organizations ultimately control the computers that make up the system?

3.Logical Decentralization: Does the system present its interfaces and data as a single, unified entity?

Among these, governance decentralization is the most critical. However, blockchain decentralization does not simply mean eliminating centers. It ensures that all nodes have equal rights and obligations. If a central authority's rights and obligations are reasonably balanced and its emergence is transparent and agreed upon by all nodes, blockchain can accommodate centralization.

Banks prefer large transactions because the relative transaction costs are lower. Processing a billion-dollar transaction incurs similar personnel and costs as a ten-thousand-dollar transaction. High transaction costs make it difficult for small transactions to receive appropriate intermediary services, as costs represent a higher proportion of the transaction amount, making them unaffordable for traders. In energy transactions, large power plants' credit issues are easily resolved, but determining the creditworthiness of rooftop solar power traders is challenging. Credit remains a significant challenge in the virtual world, and blockchain offers hope for establishing credit in the internet era.

Since blockchain technology was first used to create cryptocurrency with Bitcoin in 2009, people have quickly discovered its astonishing potential applications. Beyond digital currencies, which have garnered the most attention, people have used public blockchain platforms like Ethereum or developed their own limited-user platforms for innovative applications across various industries, including finance, transactions, retail, and healthcare, creating vast possibilities.

In 2017, major oil companies such as BP, Shell, and Norway's Equinor launched VAKT, a blockchain-based energy commodity trading platform. Chevron, Total, and India's Reliance Industries later joined. VAKT replaced the traditional "paper-based" trading model with a more transparent, efficient, and cost-effective "electronic" model.

After its successful launch, the founding shareholders used VAKT for North Sea crude oil transactions. By leveraging blockchain technology, VAKT streamlined traditional reconciliation processes, improving efficiency throughout the trade lifecycle. Its goal is to expand globally and support all physical energy transactions.

VAKT's founding shareholders are also major traders in the North Sea crude oil market, accounting for 67% of offline transactions. VAKT can calculate a fairer price than Platts' pricing by weighting data from a broader market, potentially influencing global oil pricing power.

Expanding on this vision, if VAKT captures all North Sea transactions and gains pricing power, it could redefine transaction documents and laws, such as promoting globally adopted digital bills of lading. For settlement, it might use a digital currency like Libra, pegged to a basket of fiat currencies, or a USD-backed digital currency, accelerating transactions and reinforcing USD dominance in digital and commodity markets.

China's Sinochem Energy Technology Co., Ltd. has actively developed an energy trading platform using blockchain technology for oil product import and export transactions. It initiated the drafting of the Energy and Petrochemical Trading Industry Blockchain Application White Paper (Outline), advocating for deeper industry exploration of energy blockchain applications.

German energy giant Innogy, in collaboration with IoT platform Slock.it, launched a blockchain-based peer-to-peer (P2P) electric vehicle charging project. Users can locate available charging stations via the Share&Charge app, charge at nearby Innogy charging points, and pay owners based on real-time electricity prices determined by backend programs according to grid load conditions. Blockchain ensures transparency and traceability, significantly reducing trust costs. However, widespread adoption has been hindered by poor user experience, high transaction fees, and price volatility on the Ethereum platform at the time.

In the United States, approximately half of EV owners have home charging stations, totaling hundreds of thousands of units, yet they remain underutilized. If homes can be shared via Airbnb, why not charging stations? eMotorWerks introduced the bidirectional JuiceNet software platform, a blockchain-based P2P network that organizes a distributed network of EV charging stations. Users can locate and review available charging points on a map, while owners earn fees from other drivers.

eMotorWerks founder Val Miftakhov noted that home charging installations cost between 600and1,000, significantly less than the $10,000 minimum for public installations.

In 2016, UBS, Germany's RWE, and automotive technology company ZF developed a blockchain-based electronic wallet for EV owners, enabling automatic identity verification and payment for electricity, parking, and even highway tolls. This credit tool enhances business opportunities, such as renting out vehicles via electronic contracts encoded as smart contracts, automating fee collection and payment without third-party involvement. This system also supports future autonomous EV settlements, minimizing transaction costs.

In November 2018, Korea Electric Power Corporation (KEPCO) announced the development of the "Future Microgrid" project, named

"KEPCO Open MG," aiming to create an "open energy community." By integrating existing microgrid technologies with blockchain, KEPCO seeks to improve energy infrastructure efficiency and promote local hydrogen development. Its early microgrids included small-scale photovoltaic, wind, and energy storage systems, while the open microgrid will incorporate fuel cells to enhance energy independence and efficiency, reducing greenhouse gas emissions.

Blockchain also aids in tracking green energy, benefiting green certificate management. Spanish renewable energy giant Iberdrola used blockchain technology to monitor renewable energy transmission from two wind farms and a power plant to bank offices in the Basque region and Cordoba. Leveraging an open-source blockchain platform from the Energy Web Foundation, Iberdrola aimed to meet regulatory, operational, and market demands in the energy sector. Blockchain streamlines the issuance of energy origin certificates, enabling customers to verify their energy sources. This distributed solution eliminates intermediaries, enhancing transparency and reducing operational costs. The pilot technology can also improve petrochemical product certification, saving up to €400,000 annually.

The Rocky Mountain Institute analyzed several blockchain applications in the energy sector and predicts more disruptive applications will commercialize globally in the coming years (Figure 3-10).

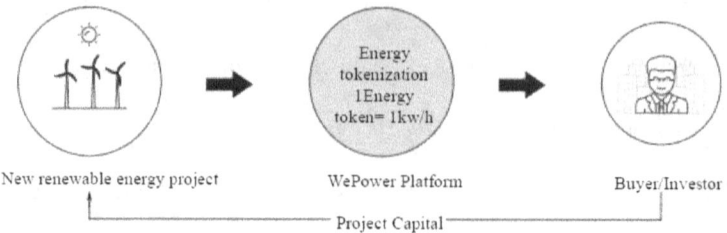

New renewable energy project   WePower Platform   Buyer/Investor

Project Capital

Figure 3-10 Schematic Diagram of Blockchain Application in

Renewable Energy Asset Trading (Source: WePower)

Note: Blockchain technology can also facilitate investment in renewable energy. The platform established by WePower evaluates the asset value of new renewable energy projects through energy tokens, thereby securing investments.

Blockchain's applications in energy are expanding. UK-based startup 4NEW introduced virtual currency into electricity trading, linking its KWATT cryptocurrency to electricity generated by a waste-to-energy plant. The plant generates 10 MWh per hour, supporting the annual issuance of 150 million KWATT tokens, with each token representing approximately 2 kWh.

De Ceuvel in Amsterdam, Netherlands, is renowned as a clean technology park established in 2012, attracting startups, artists, and residents worldwide. The park features creative studios, an auditorium, greenhouses, cafes, a B&B, and rental housing, soon to include an organic waste treatment station for local biogas production. It serves as a testing ground for sustainable living concepts, with new technologies poised for broader adoption (Figure 3-11).

Figure 3-11 Aerial View of De Ceuvel Clean-Tech Community

(Source: De Ceuvel)

Note: There are 16 office buildings, one greenhouse, one restaurant, and one hostel, all of which are connected within a local smart microgrid through smart meters.

Currently, energy suppliers bill users based on smart meter readings, with monthly settlements via banks. With tokens and electronic wallets, suppliers and community users can settle directly, leveraging blockchain for security and transparency.

Software development company Spectral and power and gas distributor Alliander conducted a blockchain-based energy trial in De Ceuvel, creating the Jouliette energy token, named after the energy unit "joule." This marks the Netherlands' first energy token, aiming to facilitate local renewable energy management and sharing, supporting the country's goal of achieving 100% renewable energy through a decentralized and reliable energy supply.

A Perfect Match

As the microgrid in Brooklyn's community strives to facilitate peer-to-peer energy trading, bringing renewable energy transactions into the homes of ordinary people, the financial sector is also nurturing a similarly grand vision: making financial services accessible to every household.

In June 2019, Facebook released a white paper announcing the launch of Libra, a blockchain-based online currency, named after the constellation Libra. The white paper begins by stating that there are still 1.7 billion people worldwide who lack access to basic financial services, despite the fact that 1 billion of them own mobile phones and half have internet access, with even the simplest smartphones now costing as little as $40. Even in many impoverished regions of Africa, smartphones are becoming a common tool for ordinary people.

We believe that Facebook's primary goal is not solely to serve these financially underserved billions. In fact, with nearly 2.7 billion users, Facebook possesses the greatest wealth in the world. However, starting the narrative from this point is not only morally commendable but also highlights a fact: the threshold for using virtual currencies is already quite low.

A comparison between distributed energy and virtual currencies supported by blockchain technology, which is characterized by its distributed nature, reveals many similarities and complementary aspects. Both adopt distributed concepts and technological support, representing highly digitalized new phenomena. They are also bottom-up disruptors: distributed energy disrupts the centuries-old centralized or pyramid-shaped energy system, while virtual currencies disrupt the traditional pyramid-shaped financial system. If successful, such disruptions will significantly reduce transaction costs, enhance efficiency, and create immense value.

Interestingly, virtual currencies have already intersected with energy in terms of pricing, albeit through energy consumption. Although no authoritative institution has precisely calculated the global energy consumption of Bitcoin mining, it is widely acknowledged that the electricity usage is enormous. A 2018 study published in the journal *Joule* estimated that Bitcoin mining consumed at least as much electricity annually as the entire country of Ireland, approximately 24 terawatt-hours (TWh), with this figure rapidly increasing.

Due to its cheap electricity, Iceland has become a haven for virtual currency mining. Statistics indicate that energy consumption for mining in Iceland has surpassed household consumption. Some have compared the energy consumption of virtual mining to that of real-world mining operations, such as copper or gold mines, finding that virtual mining consumes more energy than many real-world mining activities. In fact, when Bitcoin's price fell below $4,000, mining ceased in many regions with high electricity costs because the price was no longer sufficient to cover electricity expenses, making energy costs a benchmark for the value of virtual currencies. This situation seems somewhat absurd, leading some experts to claim that virtual currencies will have a negative impact on global climate change (Figure 3-12).

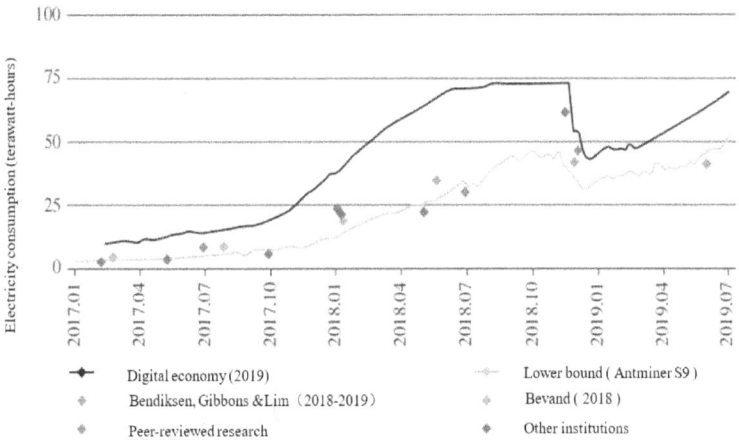

Figure 3-12 Assessment of Electricity Consumption for Virtual Currency Mining (Source: IEA)

Note: This chart presents the evaluations by IEA experts comparing electricity consumption estimates for virtual currency mining from different institutions and experts. Despite certain variations, all assessments indicate a colossal amount of electricity being used. This consumption surpasses the total electricity consumption of Ireland (26 terawatt-hours) and is even comparable to that of electric vehicles, with the global electricity consumption of electric vehicles in 2018 amounting to only 58 terawatt-hours.

The electricity consumption of virtual currencies primarily stems from the massive computations required by servers to form new virtual currencies using hash algorithms, as well as cooling systems for data centers. The location of mining operations depends on multiple factors, primarily electricity prices, but also including high-speed internet connectivity, cool climates (to reduce cooling-related electricity consumption), and, of course, local regulatory leniency and friendliness. Based on these factors, China, Iceland, Norway, Georgia, and Quebec have emerged as major mining hubs.

Regarding Bitcoin, approximately 60% to 70% is mined in China, mostly in remote regions with cheap hydro and wind power. It is estimated that 80% of mining rigs are located in Sichuan, where small hydropower is abundant and inexpensive. Some experts believe this has, to some extent, absorbed excess electricity.

Most mining sites globally utilize relatively "green" electricity. For instance, Iceland relies 100% on renewable energy, Norway 98%, and Georgia 81%. An analysis tracking 93 mining regions found that 76% of electricity consumption came from renewable sources.

Linking the value of virtual currencies to electricity consumption is clearly a distortion; they should not be indirectly connected in this manner.

As mentioned earlier, there are already better ways to establish a direct bridge between energy and virtual currencies.

However, linking virtual currencies with energy presents numerous challenges that require careful consideration and meticulous design. These challenges arise from at least two dimensions: the inherent characteristics of energy and virtual currencies, and external regulatory issues.

Electricity prices are inherently unstable and highly volatile, fluctuating more frequently than oil prices. While oil prices also fluctuate, they generally exhibit relative stability during normal periods, with predictable correlations to extraction costs and supply and demand. In contrast, electricity prices can vary by an order of magnitude within a single day. If virtual currencies are tied to energy, they must address this instability. On the positive side, although energy prices fluctuate significantly at different times, these fluctuations follow predictable patterns, not only seasonally but also daily. By incorporating big data weather forecasts (changes in wind and solar resources), the value of energy becomes more predictable. From a broader perspective, energy, including electricity, prices demonstrate greater stability over time. Cao Yin suggests that instead of linking power tokens to production, which is unstable, they could be tied to the consumption side, especially for consumers with long-term power purchase agreements. Market mechanisms could then regulate supply and demand.

Energy has a place of origin attribute, with significant price differences between production regions and distant consumption areas. Taking oil as an example, despite regional price variations, the Brent and WTI index systems effectively demonstrate the global unification of oil's value because low shipping costs enable global oil trade, smoothing out price differentials. However, renewable energy is primarily local; for instance, photovoltaic power in sunny Morocco is much cheaper than in rainy Britain, but Moroccan electricity cannot easily be transported to Britain. Even within a country or region, significant local disparities in electricity resources exist, and these price differentials are difficult to smooth out through large-scale trade, posing new challenges when linking virtual energy tokens.

In 2018, Power Ledger, an Australian company, released a white paper detailing its virtual energy currency scheme. They created their own energy trading tokens, which can be freely exchanged with fiat currencies, allowing for both purchases and redemptions. Through the Power Ledger platform, point-to-point direct energy trading is supported, as well as electric vehicle charging, carbon trading, microgrid management, market clearing, and other services.

Power Ledger also designed a dual-token model: POWER and Sparkz. POWER forms the top-level design of its blockchain trading platform ecosystem, universally applicable across the platform with payment and investment attributes, representing a typical encrypted digital currency.

Sparkz, linked to POWER via smart contracts, can be purchased with POWER and exchanged back. Sparkz is used for specific electricity transactions in different countries and regions.

Sparkz can be pegged to the fiat currency of any country using the platform, allowing for free exchange. For example, in Australia, one Sparkz equals one Australian cent, seamlessly converting with local electricity prices. POWER, akin to a global encrypted digital currency transcending national sovereignty, resembles Bitcoin. POWER tokens can be used to purchase Sparkz tokens, which, in turn, support local electricity transactions and can be exchanged for local fiat currencies. The white paper does not elaborate on the exchange rules between these two tokens, but the goal is to better facilitate the matching of energy and digital currencies (Figure 3-13).

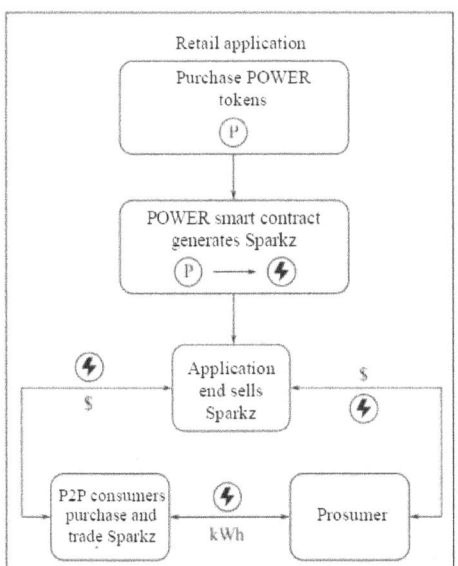 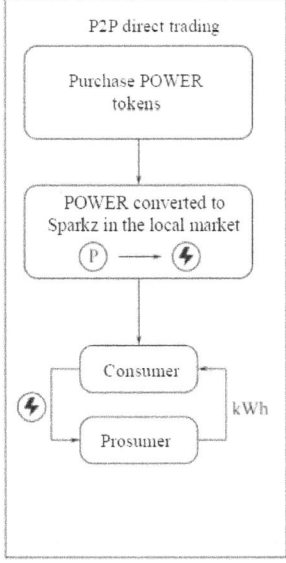

Figure 3-13 Schematic Diagram of POWER and Sparkz Applications

(Source: Power Ledger White Paper)

The integration of virtual currencies and energy is already flourishing in many places, bringing numerous new issues and, of course, more solutions. Theoretically, virtual currencies do not require an anchored equivalent, much like the gold standard is a relic of the past. However, for a currency to prevail globally, the scale of settlements conducted in it must be sufficiently large, enhancing its creditworthiness. From this perspective, if more and more energy transactions adopt virtual currency settlements, a solid foundation for spot transactions is established. Modern financial markets can then develop futures and corresponding financial products based on these spot transactions, with relatively easy standardization of energy futures products. This could potentially amplify transaction volumes tenfold or a hundredfold, fully supporting a new virtual currency system.

Regulatory issues are unavoidable. Due to regulatory challenges, early encrypted virtual currencies may need to be pegged to fiat currencies like the US dollar, although this pegging could also be more diversified. The introduction of Libra has sparked renewed debate, with public statements from Trump, the Federal Reserve, Congress, and the Securities and Exchange Commission expressing more concern than support. However, much of this concern seems rooted in misunderstanding, such as accusations of facilitating illegal transactions. Zhang Guobao, the former director of the National Energy Administration, posed an intriguing question: When buying drugs, would people prefer cash transactions or WeChat Pay? The answer is self-evident. Virtual currencies, with their identity tracking and high transparency, can actually prevent illicit transactions in many ways. Bitcoin transactions are already more transparent than many bank transactions because most digital currency exchanges have strict KYC (know-your-customer) requirements, and due to Bitcoin's traceability and immutability, tracking illegal digital currency transactions is straightforward.

Fiat currencies are backed by national credit, whereas multinational corporations like Facebook possess creditworthiness surpassing that of many governments. If corporate-led virtual currencies eventually become global currencies, they will significantly impact traditional national governance models, greatly constraining individual governments' irrational behavior.

In cross-border trade, different currency settlements pose a major obstacle. Without a global central bank, settlements must be completed through layers of banking and financial institution proxies via the SWIFT system. The United States employs its long-arm jurisdiction mechanism to prohibit dollar-based transactions with sanctioned countries, such as Iran and North Korea, relying on this system.

The emergence of Libra could disrupt this proxy mechanism, having a revolutionary impact on the international financial system. This may be the true source of the US government's deep concerns. Of course, Libra could comply with US long-arm jurisdiction, and Facebook could prohibit users from using its official Libra wallet, but it cannot control unofficial wallets.

When Satoshi Nakamoto envisioned virtual currencies using blockchain technology, he foresaw the political implications, which were even part of his goal: making politics more open and transparent.

Libra's white paper clearly and concisely outlines the vision and features of this new virtual currency: Libra's mission is to establish a simple global currency and financial infrastructure to benefit billions of people. It will be built on secure, scalable, and reliable blockchain technology; backed by real-world assets to possess intrinsic value; and managed by the Libra Association. The white paper emphasizes a key point: unlike other mainstream encrypted currencies, Libra will be backed by real asset reserves.

As of the white paper's release, Facebook listed some founding members of the association, including well-known financial payment giants like Mastercard, Visa, and PayPal, as well as representatives from shared economy platforms like Uber. However, energy companies were not yet involved. Undoubtedly, if Libra is to be pegged to real-world assets, energy is the prime candidate. Just as the agreement between the US Secretary of

State and the King of Saudi Arabia to price crude oil in US dollars supported the dollar's strong international currency status, Zuckerberg and his colleagues may soon realize that energy is the best currency reserve.

Part IV

Where Are We Headed?

Chinese energy industry leaders and government officials have demonstrated remarkable vision and insight, being among the earliest advocates of the Energy Internet globally. In practice, building an Energy Internet and responding to financial reshaping require an open market system as a prerequisite. Without an open energy market, real-time response to price signals—a prerequisite for various business model innovations—cannot be achieved. From this perspective, understanding President Xi's "Four Revolutions and One Cooperation" highlights the enormous challenges we face.

The phrase "profound transformations unseen in a century," which has almost become a slogan, is now genuinely unfolding in the energy sector. However, this transformation will not be completed swiftly, often creating the illusion that the existing framework can be sustained with mere patches and repairs. Just as we failed to anticipate the significant impact of the shale oil and gas revolution on the energy sector, we are likely to underestimate the profound effects of the digital revolution on the same field. As the world's largest energy producer and consumer, as well as the largest producer of renewable energy, China possesses a solid material foundation. The country is also deeply advancing its energy revolution, demonstrating a resolute determination to control the increase in coal consumption and phase out outdated coal-fired power plants and other inefficient energy infrastructure, with notable progress already achieved. Nevertheless, aimless patches and repairs will lead to cumulative deviations in the path of the energy revolution, ultimately placing China in a passive and disadvantaged position in this transformative process. We often say, "Base ourselves on the present and look to the future." However, this adage should perhaps be reversed; if we fail to look to the future, our efforts to "base ourselves on the present" may become increasingly challenging.

This is not merely a matter of hard power; it also requires the cooperation of soft power, with energy market construction taking precedence. If electricity prices cannot be determined through market mechanisms, real-time electricity pricing becomes unattainable. Yet, in the tide of energy digitalization, it is market prices that serve as the baton, deftly orchestrating the production and consumption of various energy sources.

Imagine an electric vehicle fully charged at night, parked in a garage, and capable of intelligently feeding electricity back into the grid during peak hours at noon. What motivates infrastructure service providers, vehicle owners, and users to engage in such operations? Certainly not out of altruism, but rather the significant economic benefits they stand to gain. Experts have assessed that if the price differential between peak and off-peak electricity exceeds a factor of two, vehicle owners could potentially achieve free electricity usage by providing such grid services and balancing their income and expenses through this price differential. Such real-time pricing is beyond the capacity of governments to set, as even a patch of dark clouds can cause fluctuations in electricity prices—how could such variations be predetermined through human efforts?

We still have a long way to go in this regard. After a protracted reform process, China's electricity market has made substantial progress and achievements. However, the spot market remains immature, and real-time electricity pricing is difficult to implement. Without sensitive market signals, innovative applications such as distributed energy and energy storage cannot identify viable business models. On one hand, the energy system needs to continuously increase redundancy to meet peak demand and accommodate a higher proportion of variable renewable energy sources. On the other hand, potential energy efficiency remains untapped. Accelerating the marketization process is a fundamental prerequisite for advancing the energy revolution, a condition that we are still striving to establish.

The same principle applies to the marketization reform of natural gas. Natural gas and electricity exhibit high synergy. When gas prices soar, natural gas power plants can profit more by reselling the gas than by generating electricity. This ability to balance supply and demand relies on flexible market prices. Natural gas, with its good storability, holds significant potential in providing system flexibility if the mechanisms are appropriate. China's natural gas marketization reform is also entering a critical phase. The establishment of a national pipeline network company does not necessarily guarantee market-driven pricing; appropriate market design, access rules, and regulatory frameworks are all essential conditions. Considering Europe's ongoing experiments with pipeline transportation of hydrogen, natural gas infrastructure still holds considerable promise in the future energy transition.

Energy market access in China continues to face numerous implicit barriers. The long-standing fragmented landscape, while fostering specialized services in its early stages, is increasingly ill-suited to current needs. A typical example is distributed natural gas energy. During the 13th Five-Year Plan period, the government planned to construct 50 million kilowatts of such capacity, a target that fell far short of realization. The primary reason is the difficulty in connecting the electricity generated by these distributed energy sources to the grid, as grid companies are reluctant to welcome such direct competitors entering at the user side. Of course, the stated reasons are often technical or safety concerns, which are given higher priority. For a long time, heating and gas supply have operated under exclusive models, hindering new entrants. For instance, if the waste heat from distributed natural gas energy can only be sold to heating companies, economic viability becomes unattainable, let alone precise real-time regulation.

China is a nation enthusiastic about embracing new things and technologies. Blockchain technology quickly took root across the country, and despite the presence of speculation, this is an inevitable process for the rapid development of new industries. In the energy sector, companies such as Sinochem and Wanxiang have persistently utilized blockchain technology to forge new energy cooperation models. Under the leadership of Jiang Bing, State Grid Electric Vehicle Service Company has developed a virtual energy token called "Lvdou" (Green Beans), creating a more advanced service platform for EV charging transactions.

The fine-tuned control and matching capabilities in energy production and consumption enabled by digitalization require market rewards. Without profitability, even the most advanced technologies cannot be widely adopted. Marketization is the most fundamental condition, while more diverse and flexible financial services are also indispensable for the efficient operation of these industries. This represents a significant challenge we face and an ongoing transformation we are striving to promote. Under the banner of the energy revolution, we need confidence but also a heightened sense of urgency.

Epilogue

Energy, finance, and the internet are undoubtedly crucial topics, but without serving humanity and improving people's well-being, they lose their fundamental purpose. The tide of innovation inevitably brings about industrial rise and fall, fostering vitality on one hand while affecting millions of livelihoods on the other. In this journey, staying true to our original aspirations is particularly important.

In the summer of 2019, when I began writing this book, I visited the Iron Man Memorial Hall in Daqing Oilfield during a business trip. It had already become a well-known revolutionary education base, and despite the heavy rain that day, it was still thronged with visitors. In the last room of the museum, behind the bronze statue of Iron Man, there was a quote from him: "My whole life is dedicated to one thing: rapidly developing China's petroleum industry."

Individuals who aspire to excel in just one pursuit throughout their lives are becoming increasingly rare in this era, yet this does not diminish the reverence people hold for such dedication. Steve Jobs, in essence, devoted his entire life to a singular endeavor as well. As time marches on and themes evolve, the human yearning for a better life remains unchanged.

The energy revolution, surging like a storm, is poised to profoundly transform the world and impact every individual. In 2019, Daqing Oilfield celebrated its 60th anniversary. After more than half a century of exploitation, its annual crude oil production had declined from a peak of 50 million tons to around 30 million tons, with the water content in many oil wells exceeding 95%. Despite Daqing Oilfield's unwavering determination to explore new resources, I couldn't help but recall the quote cited at the beginning of this book: The Stone Age didn't end because we ran out of stones, and similarly, the age of oil won't end due to a lack of oil.

Daqing has experienced the throes of reform. More than a decade ago, during the process of separating core and auxiliary businesses, a large number of workers took to the streets and petitioned, chanting, "Descendants of the Iron Man need to eat," which directly led to a regression in reform. A decade later, amidst the global surge of a new energy revolution, a sense of tranquility pervades here, as if the energy revolution is still distant. However, changes are quietly unfolding. The advancement of digital oilfields has enabled more and more stations to operate unattended, which can be seen not so much as a reduction in job positions but as an alleviation of labor shortages. Daqing Oilfield employs over 120,000 people, and reducing redundancy has long been a major concern for successive leaders. With the peak in production now behind us, up to 5,000 employees retire annually in Daqing. Time has resolved issues beyond human design, but it requires our foresight and proactive planning.

As a significant stronghold in China's energy industry, Daqing is representative. The advent of an industrial revolution brings about earth-shaking changes, but due to the prolonged transition period, the social impact is not as intense as imagined, providing ample time for digestion. Therefore, with proper arrangements and no major policy missteps, unnecessary turmoil can be avoided. China has already accumulated much successful experience in this regard.

In the 1980s, the Thatcher government took decisive action against the UK's coal industry, closing inefficient mines while enhancing mechanization in high-quality ones, leading to significant layoffs. In 1984, trade unions initiated a nationwide strike, but Thatcher, well-prepared and uncompromising, demonstrated her iron-fisted approach, even leading to a bloody conflict known as the "Battle of Orgreave." The strike ended with miners returning to work unconditionally, marking a significant political victory for the Thatcher government. In 1985, the UK government ultimately closed 25 unprofitable state-owned mines and privatized all mines by 1994. Beyond its political implications, this swiftly propelled the UK further towards a cleaner natural gas era. Nevertheless, numerous novels and screenplays have since been written on this subject, with the plight of the workers garnering widespread sympathy.

The British have continued to learn and evolve. The UK government announced that all coal-fired power plants would be shut down by 2025. Even without this ultimatum, coal-fired power plants have been struggling, with their annual operating hours hitting new lows in recent years. However, this raises a significant question: How should the old coal-fired power plants be disposed of? And behind that lies the issue of relocating potentially unemployed workers.

In recent years, we have heard numerous reports of domestic coal-fired power plants going bankrupt, from south to north, no longer isolated incidents. Even a few years ago, this would have been unimaginable, when ensuring power supply was a crucial condition for national economic development. Although the bankruptcy of these coal-fired power plants stems from various unique reasons, they are deeply imprinted with the mark of the times.

This scenario is also global. Facing increasingly challenging external development conditions, the Drax power plant in the UK invested £700 million in energy conversion, transforming into a biomass and natural gas power plant. It constructed four spherical domes, each 50 meters high, for on-site storage of biomass fuel. Sixteen covered freight trains arrive daily, transporting wood pellets to ensure an adequate fuel supply.

Currently, the generating capacity of the transformed Drax power plant remains unchanged, with both its coal-fired and biomass-fired generating capacities at 2 million kilowatts. It now has four biomass-fired generating units, with the remaining two ultimately converting to natural gas.

Drax power plant aims to serve as an innovative model, demonstrating how to revamp an aging coal-fired power plant. It also plans to build large-scale batteries within the plant to provide backup peak-shaving capacity for the grid.

Numerous other ideas exist for repurposing former coal-fired power plants. Hydrostor, a Canadian company, has designed a scheme to convert old coal-fired power plants into compressed air storage facilities. When electricity is needed, the air can be released to restart the plant's turbines. Google, meanwhile, has transformed an old coal-fired power plant in Alabama into a data center.

These cases illustrate that coal-fired power plants can find new paths for survival after coal cessation. Utilizing these aging plant resources requires wisdom, environmental awareness, and the willingness to bear necessary costs.

Energy is one of the most vital components of social life, but it must undoubtedly be examined within the broader context of the entire economic and social landscape. Throughout history, energy has often been monopolized by oligarchs, becoming a tool for a few to gain power and even enslave others. The unfolding new energy revolution will bring about many fundamental changes, one of its main features being its grassroots nature, which will inevitably flatten the pyramid-shaped energy structure. Some scholars aptly refer to this as the "democratization" of energy.

However, this "path to democracy" is destined to be fraught with challenges. As discussed in this book, distributed renewable energy must closely integrate with financial innovations represented by blockchain to complete the new round of energy revolution, greatly expanding the connotations and extensions of energy and finance, thereby profoundly impacting human society.

The allure of financial power is immense, and the competition surrounding this process will be fierce. The unprecedented convergence of the energy, information, and financial sectors will also bring unprecedented cooperation and competition. As is well known, these major fields attract the brightest minds, capable of both harnessing the greatest wisdom and producing speculators akin to evil knights attempting to achieve "righteousness" on their own terms.

Blockchain itself is not flawless, with many issues yet to be resolved. Numerous technical improvements are needed to meet the demands of massive transactions. Furthermore, as a technology that significantly enhances transaction efficiency, it is, ironically, energy-intensive. The emerging industry of "mining" spawned by blockchain is substantially increasing energy consumption, which is more about destroying wealth than creating it.

Technology, business models, and regulatory policies are the three pillars driving the energy revolution, none of which can be overlooked. Technology forms the foundation, appropriate business models enable widespread adoption, and corresponding regulation is indispensable. Virtual finance, thousands of distributed entities, and information security pose headaches for governments even individually; combined, they test the governance capabilities of every government.

An open-minded government attitude is essential. Historical progress is inevitable, and every industrial revolution relies on policy support. International competition will also unfold covertly at the industrial policy level before quickly becoming apparent. The past one to two decades have seen governments worldwide vying to subsidize renewable energy as evidence. It is under such a competitive policy environment that research, development, and investment have experienced extraordinary growth. Although governments often accuse each other of excessive subsidies and unfair competition on international stages, they all understand that, like in a race, everyone is striving to stay ahead. Of course, beyond competition, the new energy revolution also offers broader opportunities for international energy cooperation. As the saying goes, "technology knows no borders." From past competition for energy resources to future emphasis on sharing technology for local renewable energy development, the concept of a global community with a shared future will be better reflected in the energy sector.

In this new round of energy transformation, I have sensed this fervent atmosphere. The German government has held the "Energy Transition Dialogue" for five consecutive years, with attendance reaching new heights each time. Besides energy ministers from major countries, thousands of new energy enterprises use this platform to showcase themselves and strive for broader markets. The energy transition serves as a banner of morality, waving proudly as the industrial army conquers global markets.

Soft power and hard power are interconnected; one might even argue that soft power is the more crucial capability. Small countries like Denmark, as leaders in energy transition, have produced internationally renowned multinational corporations such as Vestas and Danfoss. A local government official once told me that, based on Denmark's reputation for promoting energy transition and services, the government specifically invited Danes to plan and advise on energy services. Subsequently, Danish companies undertook the renovation of the entire city's heating system, utilizing previously wasted energy and achieving excellent social and economic benefits. The project became an international demonstration project. While he spoke with pride, I thought to myself that the Danes are truly savvy businesspeople, worthy of emulation.

As I complete this book, the COVID-19 pandemic is ravaging the globe, oil prices have plummeted, and the global economy has significantly contracted, casting a dark shadow over the future. Throughout human history, every crisis has also given birth to new opportunities. During the fight against the pandemic, digital technology has played an irreplaceable role, and in the foreseeable future, this trend will profoundly impact more industries, including energy. The pandemic is also accelerating changes in people's perceptions and lifestyles, elevating the importance of the environment and health to new heights. A greener and more environmentally friendly energy system is not just a vision but is increasingly becoming a necessity.

Jeremy Rifkin argues that the Third Industrial Revolution will inevitably alter power dynamics. The First and Second Industrial Revolutions adopted vertical structures, favoring centralized, top-down management systems with power concentrated in the hands of a few industrial giants. However, the organizational model of the Third Industrial Revolution is markedly different, featuring a flattened structure where countless small and medium-sized enterprises across the country and even globally collaborate with international giants. This shift from a pyramid to a flattened power structure will not only transform our business logic but also have profound implications for culture and politics. This change can be compared to the impact of the internet on our lives, perhaps even more far-reaching.

Are we prepared?

Acknowledgments

This book covers a wide range of topics, and in many respects, I can be considered a layman. I wrote this book with the hope of providing a focal point for in-depth discussions on the future development directions of the energy sector, aiming to stimulate further exploration and insights.

I am incredibly fortunate to have had the opportunity to work at the National Energy Administration and the International Energy Agency for extended periods. These experiences not only provided me with excellent training but also offered me an exceptional vantage point from which to observe and contemplate the future of energy development. I sincerely thank my colleagues at the National Energy Administration and the International Energy Agency for their invaluable assistance, support, and encouragement.

After completing the draft of this book, a number of distinguished individuals took time out of their busy schedules to review it and offer invaluable feedback. These include Academician Jin Zhijun, Founding Dean of the Peking University Institute of Energy; Academician Du Xiangwan, former Vice President of the Chinese Academy of Engineering; Dr. Chen Xinhua, President of the Beijing International Energy Experts Club; Dr. Zhai Yongping, Energy Director of the Asian Development Bank; Cao Yin, Founding Partner of the Energy Blockchain Laboratory; Yu

Yingjiao, Vice President of Sinochem Energy Technology; Che Wei, Vice President of Danfoss China; Li Ping, Senior Vice President of NextDecade (USA); Ren Xianfang, Senior Analyst at Shell; Yao Yu, Senior Expert at the National Information Center; Mark, Executive Editor-in-Chief of Caijing Magazine; and Feng Liwen, Founder of China Energy Network. Their guidance significantly enhanced the quality of this book.

I would like to express my special gratitude to Petroleum Industry Press for their strong support. Thanks to the encouragement and support of General Manager Zhang Weiguo and Director Lang Dongxiao, this book was finally published. I also thank Ms. Tang Jing for her assistance in editing the book and redrawing the charts.

Finally, I would like to extend my heartfelt thanks to my wife, who has been my soulmate and provided me with the best spiritual support. I also dedicate this book to my sons, hoping that the future you inherit will be made even brighter by the efforts of our generation today.

References

[1] Jeremy Rifkin. The Third Industrial Revolution. Beijing: CITIC P ublishing Group, 2012

[2] Zou Caineng, et al. New Energy. Beijing: Petroleum Industry Press, 2019

[3] Robert Hefner III. The Grand Energy Transition. Beijing: CITIC Publishing Group, 2013

[4] Chen Xinhua. Decentralization is the Inevitable Trend of Energy Development. http://www.sohu.com/a/339338680_825427, 2019

[5] Qu Yongping. Three Thoughts on Global Low-Carbon Energy Tra nsition. http://www.sohu.com/a/307195284_825427, 2019

[6] Marco Alvera, Generation H, Healing the Climate with Hydrogen, Mondadori, Italy, 2019

[7] IEA. World Energy Prospects for Decentralized Energy in China. Beijing: Petroleum Industry Press, 2017

[8] Li Junfeng: Technological Innovation is the Biggest Driving Force for Energy Transition, http://guangfu.bjx.com.cn/news/20191015/10133 03.shtml, 2019

[9] Jin Zhijun, Bai Zhenrui, Gao Bo, Li Maowen. Is China Welcomin g a Shale Oil and Gas Revolution? Petroleum and Natural Gas Geolo gy, 2019, 40(3): 451-458

[10] Petroleum Observation. Only Obsolete Ideas, No Obsolete Energy: G lobal Energy Evolution and Trends—Thoughts of Academician Zou Caine ng from the Chinese Academy of Sciences on Energy Issues, 2019

[11] Merlinda Adoni, Valentin Robu, David Flynn, Simone Abram, D ale Geach, David Jenkins, Peter McCallum, Adrew Peacock, Blockcha in technology in the energy sector: a systematic review of challenges and opportunities, Renewable and Sustainable Energy Reviews 100 (2 019)143 - 174

[12] IEA, World Energy Outlook 2018, OECD/IEA Paris

[13] IEA, Digitalization and Energy, 2017, OECD/IEA Paris

[14] IEA, The Future of Hydrogen, 2019, OECD/IEA Paris

[15] IEA, Energy Efficiency 2018, OECD/IEA Paris

[16] BP, BP Statistical Review of World Energy, 2019

[17] LO3 Energy, LOCAL ENERGY SOLUTIONS, https://lo3energy.com/

[18] Claudia Pavarini, Battery storage is (almost) ready to play the fl exibility game, February 2019, https://www.iea.org/commentaries/battery -storage-is-almost-ready-to-play-the-flexibility-game

[19] China Photovoltaic Industry Association. Roadmap for the Develo pment of China's Photovoltaic Industry (2018 Edition), 2018

[20] Feng Qingdong. Energy Internet and Smart Energy. Beijing: Chin a Machine Press, 2015

[21] Fast Company, THE WORLD'S MOST INNOVATIVE COMPAN IES 2018 HONOREES BY SECTOR, https://www.fastcompany.com/mo st-innovative-companies/2018/sectors/energy

[22] Brooklyn Microgrid, Brooklyn Microgrid (BMG) is an energy market place for locally generated, renewable energy, https://www.brooklyn.energy/

[23] Facebook, the White paper of Libra, https://libra.org/en-US/white-paper/

[24] WePower, the White paper of WePower, https://wepower.network/ media/WhitePaper-WePower_v_2.pdf

[25] Denise Quirk, How Blockchain is Contributing to a More Energ y-Sufficient World With its Revolutionary Applications, Feb, 2019 http s://hackernoon.com/how-blockchain-is-contributing-to-a-more-energy-suffi cient-world-with-its-revolutionary-51a4debd6bd0

[26] Sonal Patel, Blockchain Pilot Shows Promise for Grid Balancing, June 2019 https://www.powermag.com/blockchain-pilot-shows-promise-for-grid-balancing/

[27] Office of Energy Efficiency & Renewable Energy, DOE, Consumer vs Prosumer: What's the Difference? https://www.energy.gov/eere/articles/consumer-vs-prosumer-whats-difference MAY 11, 2017

[28] Apple News, Apple now globally powered by 100 percent renewable energy, https://www.apple.com/sg/newsroom/2018/04/apple-now-globally-powered-by-100-percent-renewable-energy/ April, 2018

[29] Liu Yuanling. Change and Constancy: Trump's Climate Policies and Actions in the United States. http://117.128.6.28/cache/ias.cass.cn/ncgyj/xkfl/mgjj/201905/

[30] Liu Huo. UK: 114 Consecutive Hours of Coal Abandonment, Over 1,800 Hours of Annual Coal Abandonment. https://news.solarbe.com/201905/11/306981.html 2019

[31] Xu Fenghua, Jiang Lingao. Jinhua, Zhejiang Creates a New Model of "Pension + Wealth Management" for Photovoltaics. People's Daily. http://zj.people.com.cn/GB/n2/2016/0713/c186327-28655951.html 2016

[32] BBC news, Solar power deal will lower social tenants' energy bills. https://www.bbc.com/news/business-41122433

[33] Brian Milligan, The town where one in ten have opted for solar power, May, 2015. https://www.bbc.com/news/business-32782324

[34] Michael Köttner, Overview Biogas & Micro Scale digestion (MS D) in Germany. http://www.bioenergyfarm.eu/wp-content/uploads/2016/0 2/BEF2_151013_Micro-Scale-Digestion.pdf, 2016

[35] The National news, Noor Abu Dhabi solar plant begins commerc ial operation. https://www.thenational.ae/uae/environment/noor-abu-dhabi-solar-plant-begins-commercial-operation-1.880723

[36] Nissan Sverige officiella pressrum, Nissan supports world's first f ully commercial vehicle-to-grid hub in Denmark. https://sweden.nissann ews.com/sv-SE/releases/release-426223358-nissan-supports-world-s-first-f ully-commercial-vehicle-to-grid-hub-in-denmark, 2018

[37] UK Power Networks and Innovate UK, V2G GLOBAL ROADT RIP: AROUND THE WORLD IN 50 PROJECTS. https://www.evcons ult.nl/en/v2g-a-global-roadtrip/, 2018

[38] Deng Zhenghong. Shale Strategy—Federal Reserve in Action. Be ijing: Petroleum Industry Press, 2017

[39] Qiu Lishi. Trends and Frontier Applications of Energy Digitalizat ion. "Energy Intelligence Research", March 2019. http://www.ecsn.com. cn/news/show-723123.html

[40] Pieter Vingerhoets, Maher Chebbo, Nikos Hatziargyriou, EUROP EAN TECHNOLOGY PLATFORM FOR SMARTGRIDS-DIGITAL EN

ERGY 4.0 https://www.etip-snet.eu/wp-content/uploads/2017/04/ETP-SG-Digital-Energy-System-4.0-2016. pdf 2016

[41] KEN SAKAKIBARA, Blockchain-manged energy grid to be teste d in Fukushima, https://asia.nikkei.com/Business/Blockchain-manged-energy-grid-to-be-tested-in-Fukushima

[42] Power Ledger, Power ledger white paper https://www.powerledger.io/wp-content/uploads/2019/05/power-ledger-whitepaper.pdf 2019

[43] 4NEW, INTRODUCING THE KWATT COIN, https://4new.io/wp-content/themes/4new/images/whitepaper.pdf

[44] Grid Edge, Case Study: Artificial Intelligence for Building Energ y Management Systems, 2019, June https://www.iea.org/articles/case-study-artificial-intelligence-for-building-energy-management-systems

[45] Scott, J, Grid Edge: Artificial Intelligence for Energy Systems, Prese ntation delivered at International Energy Agency Workshop on Modernisin g Energy Efficiency through Digitalisation, Paris, 27 March 2019

[46] Jesse Morris, Jon Creyts, Five-year disruptive application period, blockchain technology will transform the global power industry. "Fort y of the Energy Chronicles", Caijing, December 2017

[47] United Nations Environment Programme, Urban Regional Energy Report (Chinese version), http://www.districtenergyinitiative.org/sites/default/files/publications/desfullreportchinese-290520171146.pdf 2015

[48] IPEEC, Top Ten Energy Efficiency Best Available Technologies and Best Practices Task Group, https://ipeec.org/upload/publication_related_language/pdf/1226.pdf

[49] Stephen Woodhouse, Chief Digital Officer, Digitalisation in the Energy Sector, https://www.poyry.com/news/articles/digitalisation-energy-sector, May 2018

[50] William Pentland, A Review Of Ted Koppel's 'Lights Out!', https://www.forbes.com/sites/williampentland/2016/04/24/a-review-of-ted-koppels-lights-out/#2bc26dd33ecc April 2016

[51] Lu Shitong, Hao Han. Innovative finance boosts energy efficiency in US building energy efficiency market, "Thirty-five of the Energy Chronicles", Caijing, July 2017

[52] Marcus Eichhorn, Mattes Scheftelewitz, Matthias Reichmuth, Christian Lorenz et al. Spatial Distribution of Wind Turbines, Photovoltaic Field Systems, Bioenergy, and River Hydro Power Plants in Germany, Data 2019, 4(1), 29 https://www.mdpi.com/2306-5729/4/1/29/htm

[53] David Roberts, Got Denmark envy? Wait until you hear about its energy policies. https://www.vox.com/2016/3/12/11210818/denmark-energy-policies

[54] Matt Kennedy, Abu Dhabi throws the switch on world's largest single-site solar project https://newatlas.com/abu-dhabi-worlds-largest-single-site-solar-project/60463/

[55] Lu Wu'an. Reshaping Energy. Hunan: Hunan Science and Technology Press, 2014

[56] Department of the Environment and Energy, Australian Government, National Energy Analytics Research program, https://www.energy.gov.au/government-priorities/energy-data/national-energy-analytics-research

This book introduces, in plain and accessible language, the current situation and development trends of the global energy transition. As people's awareness rises and lifestyles transform, a greener and more environmentally friendly energy system is not just a vision but increasingly becoming an urgent necessity.

Drawing on numerous concrete practices from both domestic and international contexts, this book elucidates the progress of the "Third Industrial Revolution" in the energy sector. It also explores the applications of blockchain technology in energy and energy finance, offering a glimpse into the brand-new landscape that these transformations will bring to future energy systems.

This book can serve as a reference for the public to understand and participate in energy transition and related policy formulation, as well as a guide for investors to grasp trends and undertake specific actions.